MANAGING PEOPLE, CULTURE AND DATA IN THE MODERN ORGANIZATION

Jaclyn Lee is the Chief Human Resources Officer of Singapore University of Technology and Design. She holds the IHRP Master Professional Certification. She is an award-winning and well-recognized HR leader with over twenty years of experience, covering the full spectrum of HR in Singapore and across Asia-Pacific. She is frequently invited to speak at local and international conferences. She is a recipient of the Public Administration Medal (Silver) for her contributions to higher education. Her first book is on accelerating organizational culture change.

Jovina Ang is the Managing Director of Communicatio and formerly an award-winning corporate executive of multiple Fortune 500 companies including Microsoft, Dell and Cisco Systems. She launched Singapore's first inter-company mentoring programme for emerging leaders in the IT industry. She has previously authored three books on leadership communication, career sponsorship and the university landscape in Singapore. She is an accredited mentor and volunteer at the Global Mentor Institute, helping under-privileged and refugee students in their job searches.

Managing People, Culture and Data in the Modern Organization

Jaclyn Lee and Jovina Ang

BUSINESS
An imprint of Penguin Random House

PENGUIN BUSINESS

USA | Canada | UK | Ireland | Australia
New Zealand | India | South Africa | China | Southeast Asia

Penguin Business is part of the Penguin Random House group of companies
whose addresses can be found at global.penguinrandomhouse.com

Published by Penguin Random House SEA Pte Ltd
9, Changi South Street 3, Level 08-01,
Singapore 486361

First published in Penguin Business by Penguin Random House SEA 2022

Copyright © Dr Jaclyn Lee and Dr Jovina Ang 2022

ISBN 9789814954709

Typeset in Garamond by MAP Systems, Bangalore, India

www.penguin.sg

ADVANCE PRAISE FOR *MANAGING PEOPLE, CULTURE AND DATA IN THE MODERN ORGANIZATION*

'This book on people, culture and data is an important contribution to managing change and leadership in this era of many unexpected events and rapid change. Authors Jovina Ang and Jaclyn Lee have argued their points very clearly and have provided clear frameworks on managing people, culture and data management for the modern organization.

I particularly like the chapters "What Got You Here Won't Get You There" and "Looking through the Future Lens". I highly recommend this book to all leaders and managers.'

—Michiel Verhoeven,
Managing Director, SAP, UK and Ireland

'There is much written about the specific topics of people, culture and data. Authors Jovina Ang and Jaclyn Lee bring all three together in a practical, linked manner supported with case studies and numerous anecdotes that provide rich insights and actionable takeaways.

This book is an important, timely read for leaders and managers alike across the organization as they look for ways to successfully navigate the ever-changing workplace, attract and retain talent and drive an inclusive culture.'

—Barbara Noonan,
Former CEO, Grid Solutions, Asia Pacific, China & Japan,
GE Renewable Energy

'This book is a treasure trove for all leaders, managers and board directors. It is filled with lots of great ideas, practical examples and case studies for leaders to build an aspirational and data-centric culture. It also shows in detailed steps how leaders can manage people, culture and data effectively in this age of rapid disruptions.

I have read the book in detail—it is very engaging, fast-paced, easy to read and so relevant to the current situation. I strongly recommend this book.'

—Daniel Teo,
Chairman, Industrial & Services Co-Operative Society Ltd
(ISCOS); Non-Executive Director and Chair of
Risk Committee, Prudential Assurance

'This book is a much-needed read for leaders and managers who are going through rapid changes in their organizations as a result of digital transformation and the pandemic. The authors have provided an extensive background and context of the challenges faced by modern organizations, and how the successful integration of culture, people and data helps provide a competitive advantage.

The practical examples, step-by-step instructions, as well as the international and local case studies give the modern manager a toolkit to manage in this complex world. Finally, the book is an easy read and provides invaluable guidance to leaders as they ponder and apply the knowledge to their organizations.'

—David Green,
Co-author of *Excellence in People Analytics*, Managing
Partner at *Insight222* and host of the
Digital HR Leaders Podcast

'This is an illuminating and practical book for all leaders and managers of the twenty-first century. There are lots of practical examples that leaders can "borrow" for their respective organizations. Every chapter has been carefully crafted to highlight the key points on how to effectively manage people, culture and data to drive organizational success for today and tomorrow. This is a must-read for all.'

—Dr Philip C. Zerrillo,
Professor of Marketing, J.L. Kellogg Graduate
School of Management and
Thammasat University, Thailand

'The post-pandemic world has created a new normal. Together with digital transformation, they have transformed organizations and the workplace. All of a sudden, we see employees working from home. This book considers some of the broader implications of workplace environment due to digitalization and the pandemic. The authors offer interesting insights into the three building blocks of organizations: culture, people, and data, and into future-proofing businesses. As culture is an immutable source of human action, the four case studies draw upon the best practices from top employers in the world to create a people-centric and data-driven culture to drive organizational performance. Every reader will learn something from this book.'

—Dr Kiat Seng Yeo,
Associate Provost and Professor, Singapore
University of Technology and Design

'Two words describe *Managing People, Culture and Data in the Modern Organization*—expansive and ambitious. Through curated research and lived experiences, Jovina and Jaclyn bring to life the key themes of a disrupted/disrupting world of work and organizations, and what it would take to navigate this modern era and not get "smashed on the rocks".

While the title suggests that the book might appeal to HR practitioners, this is far from its intent and content. With increasing digitalization and data-lisation, the underlying fabric of the modern economy is information and knowledge management, and this hinges, to a large extent, on the role that humans play in it. We each have a personal stake in this endeavour—as employers, employees, leaders, managers or supervisors—and this book highlights everyone's concerns.

Each chapter of the book ends with an 'Implications' section, which is particularly useful. It reflects the authors attempt to establish meaningful guard-rails for the modernization of organizations and the work lives of their employees, and provides a jump-pad for deeper and necessary conversations for all stakeholders.'

—Dr Eric Sandosham,
Founder and Partner, Red & White
Consulting Partners LLP

'This new book by Jovina Ang and Jaclyn Lee makes it clear that all HR professionals must be fluent not just in culture and people, but also in data, if the objective is to be effective at improving individual performance, enhancing employee experience and helping to achieve business goals.

There is no shortage of data for HR professionals. From recruitment data to promotions, productivity, absenteeism, timesheets, expenses and retention metrics, data that can be used to craft better workforce strategies is being created every day. Yet, many HR leaders struggle to realize the power of people analytics, choosing instead to rely on instinct and experience. If HR really wants to be a strategic business partner, it needs to speak with data and this book explains how to get there from here.

Readers of this book will want to become more analytical to keep pace with the new world order and be an integral part of a more data-driven, yet human-grounded future of the HR profession.'

—Dr Fermin Diez,
Author of *Fundamentals of HR Analytics*;
Deputy CEO and Group Director,
Sector Capability and Transformation Group,
National Council of Social Service (NCSS)

'I highly recommend the business and HR communities to read this relevant and practical book using the critical levers of culture, people, and data to architect the modern organization. I love the insider peeks into how OCBC has transformed its organization using these effective strategies. Given the current chaos and complexities wrought by COVID-19, it is timely that progressive organizations consider a new playbook to augment their future.'

—Carmen Wee,
Board Member, Home Team Science and
Technology Agency (HTX)

'This is written like a practical playbook linking the art and science of people and organizational development; the case studies help to put concepts into practice. Will be a good read for HR professionals wanting to know where to start their transformation journey in a COVID-19-impacted workplace.'

—Christophane Foo,
Chief Human Capital Officer, Enterprise Singapore

'Whilst technology is profoundly changing today's workplaces, what will differentiate tomorrow's leading organizations from the competition will be their organizational culture and people. Intelligent use of data will support this. This book is a must-read for leaders whose organizations are starting their HR data analytics journey.'

—Karen Loon,
Non-Executive Director of various
for-profit and not-for-profit boards;
Former PwC Singapore partner

Contents

Introduction

Alibaba. DBS. Microsoft. What is the fundamental truth about these successful organizations? Answer: their success is a function of how they have managed people, culture and data.

While organizations need stand out products and services to be competitive, to *remain* competitive, organizations need much more. The much more includes how they manage culture, people and data.

Culture is not a hollow word that 'eats strategy for breakfast'. If you want ordinary people to become extraordinary people, you need a culture to bring the best out of people and data to tell you what's working and what's not. Furthermore, as a leader and a manager of your organization, you need to inculcate a growth mindset and anthro-vision, so that every employee can be inspired to get to his or her full potential and grow.

Going digital has been a focus of organizations, whether large or small, since the 1980s. Promises of better productivity, improved customer experience and reduced costs are the reasons why organizations are going digital. But going digital is not just an exercise for the Information Technology (IT) department to implement, it is very much a people journey that is centred on nurturing the right culture and quality data for making the right decisions. The push towards going digital was accelerated by the coronavirus pandemic—a process that would have taken five years or more in the normal course, was accomplished within months.

Without a doubt, the pandemic has upended our lives and work. All of a sudden, working from home is not a nice-to-have, but rather, has become a necessity for getting work done and keeping the business lights on. Leaders and managers have also been focusing on creating camaraderie and virtual bonds between employees to foster a sense of belonging.

Organizations are also leveraging data to optimize the different aspects of work. Building a data-centric organization requires careful planning and steps that tie back to the strategy.

With the mindset of 'what got you here won't get you there', reskilling and continuous learning and development have become the norm. There are many other future-proof approaches, including continuous reskilling of employees, fostering a culture of experimentation, inculcating open innovation and practising scenario-planning, as well as leveraging big data analytics.

Finally, we see the confluence of major forces, including four disruptive forces that are affecting the world of work. These disruptive forces include demographic imbalances, geopolitics, technology and economic contraction that are affecting work in a very big way.

These are some of the reasons why we believe people, culture and data are the three fundamental building blocks for leadership and management in the digital economy, with or without COVID-19.

This book is a culmination of our practical experiences and observations of how leaders and managers are managing the modern organization. We draw upon the best practices from the top employers in Asia and across the world to illustrate the proven strategies for inculcating a digital and data-driven culture for making the right decisions and getting the most out of people. Our intention is to give you suitable guidance for leading change in the modern organization. And we refer to the insights from thought leaders across the world to substantiate our arguments through out the book.

At the end of each chapter, we include a section on managerial implications because we want to leave our readers with frameworks and thought-provoking questions so that you can take the concepts and insights shared in the chapter and readily apply them to your organization.

Chapter 1

Culture, People and Data—The Three Building Blocks of the Modern Organization

COVID-19 has caused two crises in the world. First, the 'Great Lockdown' and now, the 'Great Resignation'. Organizations will now need the three building blocks of culture, people and data to future-proof their businesses.

We are working in unprecedented times. The coronavirus pandemic has taken the world by storm and disrupted every organization in the world. The great lockdown, which was imposed to curb the spread of COVID-19, saw many countries imposing some form of lockdown, which caused a ripple effect on major sectors in many economies.

Millions of workers have been retrenched, furloughed or asked to reduce their hours of work, and workers, the world over, had to adapt to working from home as well as other types of hybrid work arrangements. In addition, hundreds of thousands of businesses have collapsed or are at the brink of collapse due to the sudden massive reduction of consumption.

As mentioned by Mr. Lee Hsien Loong, the Prime Minister of Singapore, 'We are facing the greatest crisis of our generation and this is not only a public health issue, but also a serious economic, social and political problem.'[1]

Just as organizations are beginning to get used to the idea of hybrid and remote work, and adapting their processes to fit the new normal, another phenomenon has arisen. Along with widespread employees sequestered, often working alone at home with most work connections operating through technology, physically and socially isolated, with safety protocols limiting personal connection, many employees are 'throwing in the towel'. The phenomenon of 'The Great Resignation', or a spike in talent mobility is causing havoc in the world of work as employees ponder about what is important to them and make a decision to move to the organizations that fit their values.

In the latest McKinsey article entitled 'The Great Attrition',[2] it was reported that at least 15 million workers in the United States have quit their jobs since April 2021. This record pace disrupted businesses everywhere. Many companies are struggling to address the problem as they do not really

---

[1] National Broadcast, 'PM Lee Hsien Loong: Overcoming the Crisis of a Generation', Gov.sg, 7 June 2020. Available at: https://www.gov.sg/article/pm-lee-hsien-loong-overcoming-the-crisis-of-a-generation. Accessed September 2021.

[2] Aaron De Smet, Bonnie Dowling, Marino Mugayar-Baldocchi and Bill Schaninger, 'Great Attrition or Great Attraction, the Choice is Yours', McKinsey, 8 September 2021. Available at: https://www.mckinsey.com/business-functions/organization/our-insights/great-attrition-or-great-attraction-the-choice-is-yours?cid=other-soc-lkn-mip-mck-oth-2109--&sid=5488984174&linkId=131747759. Accessed September 2021.

understand why their employees are leaving in the first place. Instead of taking the time to investigate why employees are leaving, many companies are jumping to quick fixes that do not work.

The latest McKinsey survey that polled 5,774 people in Australia, Canada, Singapore, United Kingdom and United States, highlighted the top three factors driving this great resignation, of which employees said that they:[3]

- Did not feel valued by their organizations (54 per cent)
- Were not valued by their managers (52 per cent)
- Did not feel a sense of belonging at work (51 per cent).

Whereas on the contrary, senior executives may think that the main factors why employees are leaving were compensation, work–life balance and poor physical and emotional health. Thus, there is a great disconnect between the perception of the leaders and the on-ground reality.

In addition to the above factors, people are simply too tired from having to cope with the demands brought on by the pandemic and from the lack of social interaction. In my work as a Chief Human Resources Officer, I[4] have personally witnessed many employees on the brink of mental collapse as the boundaries between work and family become blurred. Many employees are also willing to quit without a job as they become more and more disenchanted and disconnected from their employing organization.

This is why the new normal calls for the need for leaders and managers to manage differently, and for organizations to review their entire employee experience and how that impacts

---

[3] Ibid.

[4] 'I' here refers to Jaclyn Lee.

the talent strategy. The ability to intertwine the employee journey with data that can drive engagement is key to organizational performance and sustainability.

One of the best examples of this is SAP, a German software company headquartered in Walldorf, Germany. The SAP people strategy is centred on the individual employee, and the employee journey and experience are customized to suit each and every individual employee. Data from the engagement surveys is continuously monitored to show that SAP is constantly listening, understanding and acting on the feedback from employees. Along with this, SAP also measures the business health culture and the leadership trust index— which is a net promoter score for each leader, at every pulse and engagement survey cycle. Consequently, this has made SAP one of the most successful companies in the world.

We have chosen to write a book on the topics of 'People', 'Culture' and 'Data', because they go hand-in-hand in a world impacted by the coronavirus pandemic, rapid digitalization and shifting people trends and demographic imbalances. The ability to seamlessly integrate all the three topics is deemed to be crucial for the success of the modern organization. People are the foundation of any organization and without their commitment, drive and passion, organizations cannot excel or succeed. In order to have a high level of employee experience (EX), there needs to be a purposeful effort that is centred around data. Tracy Maylett and Matthew Wride in their book *The Employee Experience*[5] shared that:

> 'A well-designed EX is about creating a better future, rather than focusing obsessively on keeping employees from

---

[5] Tracy Maylett and Matthew Wride, *The Employee Experience: How to Attract Talent, Retain Top Performers, and Drive Results*, (New Jersey: John Wiley & Sons, 2017).

becoming dissatisfied, through perks, employee bonuses and the like. According to design thinking, EX is not a stack of independent initiatives; it's an integrated design built into the fabric of the organization. Design thinking goes beyond problem analysis to transformation. It's the convergence of art and also science.'

Having great EX goes beyond having the ability to integrate the people strategy with data. It also requires a continual mindset and cultural shift from one that is focused on just engagement to cultivating a purposeful engagement, where EX is at the centre of the building of a high-performing organization. Figure 1.1 illustrates a systematic approach and a model where data is the lynchpin that drives people strategy, together with cultural alignment.

According to Felix Barbar and Rainer Strack,[6] before any organization can look to data to help them reconvert their business, they must first identify the fulcrums—where and

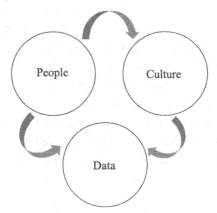

Figure 1.1: Model to Cultivate Purposeful Engagement

Source: Authors' own

---

[6] Felix Barber and Rainer Strack, 'The Surprising Economics of a "People Business"', *Harvard Business Review*, 83 (6) (2005), pp. 80–90.

how values are being created or squandered. Organizations, especially those that are focused on people-intensive businesses, need rigorous measures, similar to the measures that are used in the financial industry, to understand the productivity of people, rather than that of capital. The financial services industry uses many types of metrics, ratios and key performance indicators to accurately measure performance.

Because employees represent both the major cost and the major driver of value creation, any people management measure and move can drive changes in the organization's operational performance and impact the bottom line. As such, people-intensive businesses need measures such as employee-oriented performance metrics, to drive performance and help achieve better returns on their investments. Short-term, variable incentives and compensation schemes can further be designed to elevate performance.

In this chapter, we give an overview of people management in the post-COVID-19 world, and look at how agility and adaptability are crucial in these challenging times. We discuss the importance of a data strategy to provide insights into the employee journey. We show how organizations can future-proof themselves in a world that is increasingly becoming more volatile, uncertain, complex and ambiguous. Fundamentally, we also believe that organizations need to ask the question: Where do they want to be? COVID-19 is a reset, and past successes are no guarantee for future successes. For the rest of the book, we have also included several case studies of organizations that have successfully integrated people, culture and data to drive organizational performance.

People

The pandemic has brought the focus back on to the individual worker and the topic of employee well-being. And people management has never been more challenging than during these turbulent times.

The COVID-19 pandemic threw employers and employees into chaos and uncertainty, with no clear end in sight. HR operated in crisis mode for much of 2020 and the first half of 2021, figuring out how employees could work from home, trying to provide extra mental and physical health support, and working more than ever on C-level strategies for keeping their organizations functioning.[7]

Questions such as 'how do organizations realign culture and values in this post-pandemic world to one of inclusion, sustainability and integration?', 'How do we use employee data to design new career structures and jobs as a result of the pervasiveness of telecommuting?' and 'How do we develop leadership models and team structures that can build trust, encourage effective debate and productive conflict in this new age?' are now at the forefront of the minds of leaders and managers. These questions are keeping them awake at night.

We are also living in a world of EX 4.0, where employee satisfaction intertwines with customer satisfaction. Tracy Maylett and Matthew Wride argued in their book *The Employee Experience*, that EX is now equal to CX (customer experience).[8] The analogy that employees are the soil and nutrients in which customer experience grows, fits this picture.

In Figure 2, we show the evolution of employee experience from EX1.0 to EX 4.0.

[7] Tam Harbert, 'The Pandemic Has Expanded the Role of HR', *SHRM HR Magazine*, Fall, 1 September 2021. Available at: https://www.shrm.org/hr-today/news/hr-magazine/fall2021/Pages/pandemic-expands-role-of-hr.aspx. Accessed September 2021.

[8] Maylett and Wride, *The Employee Experience*.

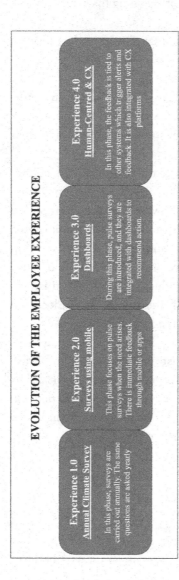

Figure 1.2: The evolution of employee experience from EX1.0 to EX 4.0

Source: Adapted from Josh Bersin, 'Employee Experience 4.0: Shortening the Distance from Signal to Action'[9]

[9] Josh Bersin, 'Employee Experience 4.0: Shortening the Distance from Signal to Action', Joshbersin.com, 13 November 2020, available at: https://joshbersin.com/2020/11/employee-experience-4-0-closing-the-loop-from-signal-to-action/. Accessed September 2021.

Also, an engaged workforce that feels respected and appreciated, will have higher levels of trust in their leaders. Thus, they are more likely to take risks and invest emotionally in the organization.

As Tony Fernandes, Group CEO of AirAsia once said: 'Employees come number one, customers come number two. If you have a happy workforce, they'll look after your customers anyway.' [10]

Thus, if you take care of EX, CX will take care of itself.

This view is also supported by Josh Bersin, a worldwide expert on all things HR. In his article 'Employee Experience 4.0', he shares,

> 'In this era we don't just send surveys to collect data: we collect signals in many forms, we analyze it in real-time, and *we send it to the right person* in the company who needs to take action. I call this the "Continuous Response" phase of EX . . . While the EX agenda may have started in HR, it now spans everything from HR to IT facilities, health and safety facilities, and even finance and legal. All these functional areas are part of the employee experience, so they all have to be part of the company-wide EX Initiative.' [11]

The theme of "employee experience" and the need for continuous feedback is the overwhelming desire—what employees are looking for. Employees want that personal connection with

[10] 'How Air Asia Founder Tony Fernandes' Dream Came True', *BBC*, 1 November 2010. Available at: https://www.bbc.com/news/business-11647205. Accessed September 2021.

[11] Josh Bersin, 'Employee Experience 4.0', Available at: https://joshbersin.com/2020/11/employee-experience-4-0-closing-the-loop-from-signal-to-action/. Accessed September 2021.

and individualised experience in the organizations that they are working for. This finding was clearly highlighted in a McKinsey article on COVID-19 and the employee experience.[12] In the survey, McKinsey showed that the pandemic and the crisis of working from home are affecting employees' daily work lives in physical, mental and emotional terms.

As more employees return to the office, we recommend that organizations rethink employee experience in ways that respect individual differences such as home lives, skills, capabilities, mindsets, personal characteristics and other factors that make the employees feel special, wanted and valued. With the proliferation of listening technologies and advancements in behavioural science, advanced analytics and other technologies, there are many tools and methods that leaders and managers can turn to, to address employee experience in a more targeted way.

Listening more to employees will help to bridge the gap between what leaders and managers think employees want and what employees actually want. Hence, employee engagement surveys, which are typically rolled out on an annual or biennial basis, will now have to migrate to continuous response action-oriented platforms, where data is continually measured.

The ability to use and look at data to customize the employee experience on a continuous basis, will be key to winning the battle for talent, which is expected to intensify. As the nature of work changes, new skills will be needed to operate in a highly digitalized, human-centric world of the Fourth Industrial Revolution. The chapters that follow will expound further on this topic.

---

[12] Jonathan Emmett, Gunnar Schrah, Matt Schrimper, and Alexandra Wood, 'COVID-19 and the Employee Experience: How Leaders Can Seize the Moment', McKinsey, 29 June 2020. Available at: https://www.mckinsey.com/business-functions/organization/our-insights/covid-19-and-the-employee-experience-how-leaders-can-seize-the-moment#. Accessed September 2021.

The latest Deloitte Global Human Capital Trends survey showed that 61 per cent of business and HR leaders face difficulties finding qualified and experienced hires.[13] As such, providing a unique, customized and individualized employee experience is key to organizational success.

Work will also become more hybrid and remote as organizations discover the cost savings that are a result of less office space. Another noticeable trend is the shift from organization-driven learning approaches to self-driven learning. Which is why there needs to be a review of employee capability data on a constant basis for organizations to plan the best way for work to be done, as well as to deploy the best workers to meet the customers' changing needs.

Employee monitoring, including the monitoring of employee sentiment, will be on the rise through the use of commonly used office tools and applications, such as Microsoft Office365. Organizations potentially can use this data to curate an individualized, consumer-like employee experience that is customized to suit their unique needs. However, as organizations continue to leverage data to improve employee experience, there is also a need to ensure data intelligence and data privacy. The delicate balance between using sensitive data and protecting employee privacy will be something which organizations have to carefully manage.

Culture in the New Normal

Integral to the topic of people in organizations is the element of culture. Culture is the factor that brings organizations together

---

[13] Deloitte, '2021 Global Human Capital Trends: Special Report', December 2020. Available at: https://www2.deloitte.com/us/en/insights/focus/human-capital-trends.html. Accessed September 2021.

and aligns their workforce to a common mission and set of values to achieve a common goal and key business objectives.

What used to work in the past might not work today, as the pandemic has brought about major disruptions in organizations and businesses. It has also reset how work is done, and redefined what employees want as the line between work and life becomes more and more blurred.

Prolonged periods of isolation are making people feel disenchanted, disconnected and losing a sense of belonging with their organizations—an important need that ranks third after one's physical and security needs on the Maslow's Hierarchy of Needs.[14] Hence, the new normal is driving a new type of revolution in organizational culture alignment and transformation as companies are being disrupted through the constant changes in the wake of the pandemic and Industry 4.0.

According to Jenny Chatman and Francesca Gino, COVID-19 could weaken the foundations of organizational culture.[15] Which is why, at the present moment, the following questions are fundamental for organizations to answer:

- Will the organizational culture take a hit as people can't meet in person, thus making it harder to solidify their shared beliefs?
- Will they be less able to use culture as a roadmap for making good decisions in a tumultuous time?

---

[14] Abraham Maslow, 'Maslow's Hierarchy of Needs', Index of DOCS/ Teacing (sp), Collection/Honolulu, 1943.

[15] Jenny Chatman and Francesca Gino, 'Don't Let the Pandemic Sink Your Company Culture', *Harvard Business Review*, 17 August 2020. Available at: https://hbr.org/2020/08/dont-let-the-pandemic-sink-your-company-culture, accessed September 2021.

- How can organizations continue to build and leverage culture while most of the organization is operating largely remotely?

Chatman and Gino also found that organizations that are strategically aligned, strong and have built the capacity to adapt quickly to dynamic environments, can earn 15 per cent more in annual revenue compared to those in the same industry that are less adaptable.[16]

Thus, cultural agility is important during these turbulent and difficult times. Organizations that demonstrate the ability to quickly change and adapt their culture to the new environment, will thrive. We call this 'future-oriented culture'.

The new work environment will require employees to adapt to the use of digital tools for communication, work and collaboration. Organizations that already have a digital-ready culture will have a distinct advantage, as they have, in essence, embraced the future of work compared to those who do not. In assessing culture in the digital age, Julie Goran, Laura LaBerge and Ramesh Srinivasan found that shortcomings in organizational culture are one of the main barriers to organizational success.[17]

There are three digital cultural deficiencies that are present in today's organization. These include:

1. Functional and departmental silos
2. Fear of taking risks

---

[16] Ibid.

[17] Julie Goran, Laura LaBerge and Ramesh Srinivasan, 'Culture for a Digital Age', *McKinsey Quarterly* 3, 2017, pp. 56–67. Available at: https://www. mckinsey.com/business-functions/mckinsey-digital/our-insights/culture-for-a-digital-age. Accessed September 2021.

3.   Difficulty forming and acting on a single view of the customer

Cultural obstacles also correlate with negative economic performance. In view of this, leaders and managers will be required to take a proactive stance in shaping and measuring culture, and approach it with the same rigour with which they tackle operational transformations.[18] And culture will be the force that brings the changes to strategy, technology, processes and structure in any digital transformation efforts.[19]

In order to accelerate culture transformation for the new normal, Namgyoo Park asserted that collaboration platforms such as Microsoft Viva, Slack, etc. are some ideas of technologies used for brainstorming, idea generation and open communication, in which ideas can be shared in real-time are vital components of success.[20] These real-time exchanges and interactions allow for faster and more efficient collaboration, which is one of the key ingredients to successful culture transformation.

The use of data to drive organizational culture transformation is vital to the process of change. So is the ability to measure the gap between the current and desired state of culture. These steps are important to begin to drive action.

---

[18] Ibid.

[19] Alyson Clarke, 'Prioritise Culture Change to Accelerate Digital Transformation', *Forrester*, 2018. Available at: https://go.forrester.com/blogs/prioritize-culture-change-to-accelerate-digital-transformation/. Accessed September 2021.

[20] Namgyoo K. Park, 'The Cultural Impact of Automation: Quality of Work and Life Redefined', *Transformation of Work in Asia Pacific in the 21st Century* (HKUST Business School and APRU, 2018), pp. 129–164.

Data can help organizations to understand the different types of gaps—whether these gaps refer to areas pertaining to leadership, people practices, empowerment, trust—among a whole host of other factors. These gaps can be turned into data points within the employee lifecycle to help leaders double down and focus on the tangible actions needed to transform culture. Ultimately, a company must be able to demonstrate the concrete impact of culture on revenue. The following chapters will expound further on these concepts.

Diving Deep into Organizational Culture

Given culture is so important, what more can we tell you about culture and its impact on organizational performance?

Kim Cameron and Robert Quinn defined organizational culture as 'the taken-for-granted values, underlying assumptions, expectations and definitions that characterise organizations and their members. It is an enduring slow-to-change core characteristic of [an] organization.'[21]

While culture is complex and not easy to crystallize, it is a critical part of the organizational glue that binds people together to a common vision and goal. In their research, Barbara Fralinger and Valerie Olson found that a strong and well-defined culture helps to pave the way for stakeholders to align their actions towards achieving an organization's vision and objectives.[22]

---

[21] Kim S. Cameron and Robert E. Quinn, *Diagnosing and Changing Organizational Culture: Based on the Competing Values Framework*, Third Edition, (San Francisco, CA: Jossey-Bass, 2011).

[22] Barbara Fralinger, and Valerie Olson, 'Organizational Culture at the University Level: A Study Using the OCAI Instrument', *Journal of College Teaching & Learning* (TLC) 4, (11) (2007). Available at: https://doi.org/10.19030/tlc.v4i11.1528. Accessed October 2021.

In my book *Accelerating Organization Culture Change*,[23] I shared a case study of how a successful CEO of a large global company demonstrated how culture and values are very much integrated. In his company of more than 10,000 employees, he has to constantly ensure that the values of employees are aligned with the culture and values of the organization. This is important, as it is the reason that customers trust the company and employees feel attracted to and have a sense of belonging to the organization. It is also the factor that holds and binds a community together. Thus, culture is a building block that needs to be built over time; it must be protected as it is something that can be fragile and easily broken.

In practice, culture can mean getting the team to be aware and apply the organizational values and actions to constantly validate it. But culture is also about internalizing and 'walking the talk'. In order to achieve the 'to be' culture and values, various levels of engagement at all levels of the organization through formal or informal communication and work systems can help with alignment and a common understanding amongst the workforce.

This common understanding helps to reinforce the notion of shared perceptions of work practices needed for organizations to succeed.[24] Given that they are shared perceptions, members of the organization can participate in the process of agreeing upon their perceptions of the current culture and define the desirable culture, while having an open dialogue to share their

---

[23] Jaclyn Lee, *Accelerating Organization Culture Change: Innovation Through Digital Tools.* Emerald Group Publishing, 2020.

[24] Peter T. Van den Berg and Celeste PM Wilderom, 'Defining, Measuring and Comparing Organizational Cultures', *Applied Psychology*, 53 (4) (2004), pp. 570–582.

individual perceptions of how to work together to achieve the desired culture.

Cultural Alignment

In order to progress in the culture journey, senior management, key stakeholders and HR professionals will need to be aware of and well-equipped with the necessary knowledge and tools to help members of the organization to achieve the desired culture change. A culture transformation cannot be done in isolation. Rather, the whole process needs to be conducted across business units, functions and levels.

As explained by KPMG,[25] COVID-19 has provided us with an opportunity to proactively ensure we do not fall back to old practices. The first challenge for leaders is to deliberately observe, reflect, capture, celebrate and reinforce elements of culture that have emerged during the crisis, that they want to keep. Second is to have deliberate dialogue with their employees to elicit their views on how they want to move forward with the culture.

When there is common understanding achieved, there will be cultural alignment. By allowing members to share their perceptions, it will drive them through a process of alignment of their perceptions of the current culture towards the desired culture.

That said, it is likely for subcultures within the organization to coexist at the different organizational units, levels and even among teams of individuals. The emergence of subcultures is due to a variety of reasons. Reasons like different personalities,

---

[25] Comac Deady, Conor McCarthy and Sinead Egan, 'Conscious Culture Creation: Seizing New Ways of Working', KPMG. Available at: https://assets. kpmg/content/dam/kpmg/ie/pdf/2020/11/ie-conscious-culture-creation-seizing-new-ways-of-working.pdf. Accessed September 2021.

motivations, goals, needs, agendas and backgrounds can nurture subcultures to flourish.

Therefore, it is also important to identify the perceptions of the key stakeholders in the various units about the organization's current and desired cultures. If the current culture and/ or subcultures are found to be different from the desired organizational culture, the organization will need to undergo a culture change exercise.

During the pandemic, sustaining culture has become fundamental to how the organization functions and survives. In her research, Kathy Gurchiek[26] found that among people managers, more than half or precisely 52 per cent, spend an average of one to ten hours weekly, managing their employer's culture, while the remainder devote twenty-one hours or more per week managing culture. Despite the hours dedicated to sustaining culture during the pandemic, it was found that 62 per cent of HR professionals said that 24 per cent of their respective overall workplace culture has worsened since the pandemic struck. Among the reasons for the worsening of culture are lack of communication and changes, and an increase in workload.[27]

One important critical success factor for sustaining organizational culture refers to the employees' ability to work across multiple teams and people with different types of skill sets and expertise in an agile manner. Furthermore, teams need to be assembled quickly to solve complex problems, which in essence, is the ethos of Scrum teams. If anything, the pandemic

---

[26] Kathy Gurchiek, 'Research: Employees Rely on Employer Culture to Navigate Pandemic', *SHRM HR Magazine*, 9 September 2021. Available at: https://www.shrm.org/hr-today/news/hr-news/pages/research-employees-rely-on-employer-culture-to-navigate-pandemic.aspx. Accessed September 2021.

[27] Ibid.

has taught us that culture agility is crucial to success and organizations that can transform fast will win the race.

As an Incident Commander and Chief HR Officer for Singapore University of Technology and Design (SUTD), I[28] had to work very quickly with the senior management team and many stakeholders on the ground to make decisions quickly in order to ensure the university is able to respond quickly to the very fluid pandemic situation. The key successes of the SUTD organization is the fluidity of the organization and a lack of bureaucracy in decision-making.

These characteristics have helped the university to respond to the employees and key stakeholders' needs in a very timely manner, thus, ensuring the safety and security of the campus while observing the social distancing rules that COVID-19 mandates. The testament as to how the university has responded in an agile way can be found in the latest employee pulse survey that indicated that 81 percent of employees felt well-supported by their supervisors and colleagues. The employees also told the university that the supervisors and colleagues had reached out frequently to show their care and concern for their welfare and well-being from the very start of the pandemic that took place in March 2020 until now.

We can see from the above sections and the SUTD example that clear communication and cultural alignment are key, and important to sustaining performance and coping with change. We will discuss the topic of data and how this lynchpin ties everything together, next.

Data

The last imperative of driving rapid change coupled with the need to improve employee EX is the utilization of data to

---

[28] 'I' refers to Jaclyn Lee here.

help organizations become more precise and purposeful in their transformation journey. At SUTD, the data culture is so pervasive that it is the first source that we turn to, to organize talent and make better decisions.

As a matter of fact, data has become so prevalent in all areas of work. Daniel Franklin wrote in his book *Mega Tech: Technology of 2050* that over the next three decades, as the techniques of artificial intelligence worm their way into all areas of life, fundamental changes are underway. Every aspect of business and society will be touched by data, just as they have been by computing and the internet over the past three decades.[29]

In today's digital economy, the need to drive data culture is an important facet of transformation. Organizations with strong data-driven cultures typically will have top managers who set the expectation that decisions must be anchored in data while they role-model and lead by example.[30]

A recent case study of a leading global and technology services company that had a headstart in building a data culture, illustrated that the company could use analytics to predict skill shortages during the pandemic. The company could also deliver seamless training in real-time while mitigating critical cyber risks and preparing for critical IT infrastructure. Consequently, the company was able to deliver sophisticated infrastructure and designs for their customers ahead of their competitors, resulting in increased customer satisfaction and company performance.[31]

---

[29] Daniel Franklin, *Mega Tech: Technology in 2050* (London: Profile Books, 2017).

[30] David Waller, '10 steps to Creating a Data-driven Culture', *Harvard Business Review*, 6 February 2020. Available at: https://hbr.org/2020/02/10-steps-to-creating-a-data-driven-culture2-7. Accessed September 2021.

[31] Anil Khurana, Roger Wery and Amy Peirce, 'Using Data to Fuel Your Business Resilience in the Post-COVID-19 World', PwC, 2 February 2021.

In developing the analytics strategy for an organization, there are several stages in the lifecycle. It begins with operational reporting, which is mainly reactive, followed by advanced reporting, which is more proactive reporting for benchmarking and decision-making. The next stage is advanced analytics, which uses statistical analysis to solve business problems and here, there is integrated data across the organization. The most advanced stage is predictive analysis, where there is development of predictive models, scenario planning and integration with strategic workforce planning. Outcomes from advanced analytics and predictive analysis will be illustrated in the ensuing case study chapters. In order to develop a very strong data culture that can harmonize with better decision-making, organizations not only have to focus on the process and integration, but also culture and talent, for which the process involves extensive use of workforce analytics.

Workplace analytics is a fundamental tool for not just improving employee experience, but ultimately, to impact business performance. As mentioned earlier, once there is EX, CX will follow. That said, for analytics tools to be effective, organizations need to pair data-derived insights with proactive and empathetic decision-making. Demonstrating and defining improvements accurately using this information is also critical. And it involves working together to connect data from across the organization into an overall benchmark, such as a net promoter score.

While the potential for data-driven insights to redefine employee experience is formidable, let us not forget that the most important consideration has to be centred on people. Making

---

Available at: https://www.pwc.com.au/digitalpulse/data-transformation-insights-coronavirus.html. Accessed September 2021.

sure employees are well-informed and feel comfortable with how workplace data is being used is paramount. Communicating transparently and showing the long-term benefits is key to fostering a trusting environment.

In his book on people analytics, Mike West highlighted the importance of the employee journey map. The employee journey map provides a one-stop-shop to see how these different concepts fit together as one: a framework, customer journey stages, employee journey stages, company touchpoints, survey feedback tools and systems feedback tools.[32]

Furthermore, people management is becoming more computational. The more data that is available, the better we can design the interventions for a great employee experience and culture. According to Mike West, people analytics should follow 'a triple A' framework that comprises 'Attraction', 'Activation' and 'Attrition'.[33] Attraction represents a set of metrics and analyzes intended to measure the attractive force of the company to acquire the quality of talent it wants. In the Activation phase, the set of metrics and analyzes measure the proportion of people and teams who have all the basic requirements to produce high performance. In the Attrition phase, the set of metrics and analyzes measure the degree of control the company has over the quality of the talent it is able to retain versus the quality of talent it allows or encourages to exit.

We believe 'People', 'Culture' and 'Data' are the three essential building blocks of the modern organization. These three building blocks are key for organizations to navigate today's volatile, uncertain, complex and ambiguous world of work that is infused with all things digital.

---

[32] Mike West, *People Analytics for Dummies*, Tantor Media, 2020.
[33] Ibid.

We hope you will find deep insights in this book that will help you with your transformation journey.

Managerial Implications

Given that people, culture and data are the imperatives of the modern organization, we would like to include managerial implications here to help readers connect with the topics discussed and assess its relevance to your respective organizations. We would recommend the following:

- Review your organizational data strategy by doing a SWOT (strengths, weaknesses, opportunities and threats) analysis, and looking at gaps and opportunities to make it more robust;
- Examine your people strategy and how teams are organized within your organizational structure. Is your organizational structure built for agility to quickly assemble and dismantle teams quickly when a crisis occurs?
- Review your current organizational culture. Does it support your organizational strategy in a post-COVID-19 world? To get the process started, here are some recommendations:
  - ° Conduct an organizational culture diagnostic to understand the gaps between current culture and the future culture, specifically the requirements that are critical to succeed in a post-COVID-19 world;
  - ° Conduct culture conversations with your people to solicit ideas for change to move towards the desired state;
  - ° Assemble the ideas and form agile project teams to work to address the gaps.

Chapter 2

COVID-19 and the New Norm of Work

Adaptability is key for navigating the hybrid and remote way of work.

COVID-19 has impacted work in more ways than one. Who would have thought a virus could bring the world to its knees and change the world of work forever? In this chapter, we elaborate the impact of the pandemic on the future of work, especially how it has affected the way in which organizations have viewed people, culture and data.

With the introduction of the 'Great Lockdown' in March and April 2020, the world of work changed forever. Before this, there had never been such a coordinated single act by governments and organizations across the world. The magnitude and speed of the cessation of activity that followed the lockdown was unlike anything that we had seen and experienced before. Almost overnight, offices and shops had to close. Parks, streets and beaches became empty as people retreated to their homes to curb the spread of the coronavirus.

In less than a week, many organizations converted their physical and face-to-face workplaces to remote working setups. Many white-collar and knowledge workers had to adapt to working from their home—in their home offices, lounges, garages and at kitchen tables, to avoid contracting COVID-19.

Just when we thought work would get back to some sort of normalcy with high vaccination rates in many developed countries, we were hit by the Delta variant in 2020.[34] By 2021, the Delta variant had made waves in India, Southeast Asia and many parts of the world. With the outbreak of the Delta variant, many countries, including Singapore,[35] were faced with the fourth wave of the pandemic. Even in October 2021, Singapore remained in a semi-lockdown mode.

By the end of 2021, another variant—the Omicron—had emerged and spread across the world. Today, at the beginning of 2022, the Omicron variant—while appearing to be milder than the Delta variant—has become the most infectious variant across the world.[36]

Which is why many workplaces have either remained closed or have been practising restricted opening hours for a

---

[34] Kathy Katella, '5 Things to Know About the Delta Variant', *Yale Medicine*, 6 January 2022. Available at: https://www.yalemedicine.org/news/5-things-to-know-delta-variant-covid. Accessed February 2022.

[35] Ben Westcott, 'Delta Variant Outbreak Threatens Singapore's Living with COVID model', *CNN*, 7 September 2021. Available at: https://edition.cnn.com/2021/09/07/asia/singapore-covid-19-restrictions-intl-hnk/index.html. Accessed September 2021.

[36] Centres for Disease Control and Prevention, 'Omicron Variant: What You Need to Know', 2 February 2022. Available at: https://www.cdc.gov/coronavirus/2019-ncov/variants/omicron-variant.html. Accessed February 2022.

select number of employees. Hybrid and remote work have become the new norm. As is the use of digital technologies and cloud-based applications, including Zoom, Teams and Google Hangouts, the Microsoft suite of tools, has increased exponentially so employees can make use of these digital technologies to perform their work tasks from home.

The emergence of the new norm of work has caused many organizations to rethink the future of work and come up with adaptation strategies to cope with the new ways of working brought on by the pandemic. It is foreseeable that remote work or some form of hybrid remote–physical work system will remain a feature of work in the future.

Studies have shown that there are still over 70 percent of people who work from home most of the time.[37] Additionally, 74 percent of organisations intend to increase remote work even well after the pandemic is over.[38]

In Singapore, where we are based, the government has been recommending work-from-home as the default mode of work.[39] Some leading organizations, including Facebook,

[37] Kim Parker, Juliana Menasce Horowitz, and Rachel Minkin, 'How the Coronavirus Outbreak Has—and Hasn't—Changed the Way Americans Work', Pew Research Centre, 9 December 2020. Available at: https://www.pewresearch.org/social-trends/2020/12/09/how-the-coronavirus-outbreak-has-and-hasnt-changed-the-way-americans-work/. Accessed July 2021.

[38] Mary Baker, '9 Future of Work Trends Post-COVID-19', *Gartner*, 8 June 2020. Available at: https://www.gartner.com/smarterwithgartner/9-future-of-work-trends-post-covid-19/. Accessed July 2021.

[39] Cindy Co, 'Work-from-Home to Remain as Default; Jobs Support Scheme Extended to July 9', *Channel News Asia*, 18 June 2021. Available at: https://www.channelnewsasia.com/news/singapore/work-from-home-wfh-default-jobs-support-scheme-covid-19-15040560. Accessed July 2021.

Google, Twitter, Mastercard and Shopify, have decided to move permanently to remote work.[40]

The Push Towards Digital Transformation

The work-from-home revolution is not a new revolution in the world of work. In fact, it has been a common mode of working for companies in the IT industry for the past thirty years.

Having worked in IT myself for the past twenty-five years, I[41] have been doing some form of remote work at many of the Fortune 500 companies where I have worked at. Companies like Cisco Systems, Dell, Microsoft and Sun Microsystems, which was acquired by Oracle, have been offering the option to work from home for employees for the past thirty years. When I worked for Sun Microsystems, I worked two days per month in the office.

The work-from-home revolution would not have been possible if not for technology. In the early 1990s, affordable personal computers and laptops that had Microsoft Word, Excel and PowerPoint pre-installed, became widely available.

In the mid 1990s, emails had become the main tool for communication between managers and employees. With Netscape's Initial Public Offering (IPO), we saw a surge in information being posted on the World Wide Web. By late 1990s, remote work had become widespread in the IT industry,

---

[40] Tang See Kit, 'Goodbye Office: Is the Future of Work in Our Homes?', *Channel News Asia*, 25 May 2020. Available at: https://www.channelnewsasia.com/news/business/goodbye-office-work-from-home-future-covid-19-12758558. Accessed August 2021.

[41] 'I' here refers to Jovina Ang.

when dot-com companies began offering this perk to attract employees to the Silicon Valley in the United States.

In the early 2000s, high-speed internet became available with the advancement of routing and switching technologies. By 2010, the introduction of smartphones further accelerated remote work. With smartphones, employees could communicate easily via the telephone and email, while at the same time, have access to the internet. Between 2010 and 2020, there were major capability advancements in video communication on the smartphone and computer laptop. Tools like Zoom, Microsoft Teams and Google Hangouts were launched to enable organizations to run remote meetings efficiently and effortlessly.

But technology would not have much of an impact if not for its widespread adoption. Many organizations have jumped on the technology bandwagon for multiple reasons, of which one primary reason is to drive productivity. Technology can lower the transaction costs for group formation and action. It can also 'shift time' as team members do not have to be in the same room at the same time to meet and collaborate— technology can facilitate easy communication with one ping, one click, one tweet or one post. The trend towards digital transformation started well before the pandemic struck. Many organizations were seen digitalizing many aspects of how they were conducting business or empowering their employees.

COVID-19 has simply accelerated the need for digital adoption at a much faster rate to 'keep the lights on' for business continuity, as well as to enable employees to work from home and interact with their customers through digital tools and platforms.

In an article published on 13 August 2021, Girija Pande and Frederic Donck shared that sustainability and digital transformation had become the top focus areas of leaders of governments and businesses across the world:

> 'It would be an understatement to say that digitalization and green transformation have become two top priorities for governments and businesses around the globe. Global spending on digital transformation could top US2.4 trillion by 2024. Digitalization has clearly streamlined existing processes, transformed many industries and is widely seen as a major bridge towards a new carbon-neutral world.'[42]

The proliferation of the internet has also created a common playground for interfacing computer platforms of different computing technologies. Which is why organizations can embrace an 'e-everything' approach to their business models and people strategies that go beyond business process reengineering.

With the commercialization of internet technologies, we also see businesses offering e-commerce as a critical component of how they interact and transact with their customers. And the growing capabilities of artificial intelligence (AI) combined with decreasing costs in cloud computing, Internet of Things (IoT) and big data analytics will lead to a new machine age[43] that is more seamless and human-like.

COVID-19 has also led organizations to use technology to reduce reliance on human beings and transform work in many

---

[42] Girija Pande and Frederic Donck, 'Digitalisation is Growing, so is its Carbon Footprint', *Straits Times*, 13 August 2021. Available at: https://www. straitstimes.com/opinion/digitalisation-is-growing-so-is-its-carbon-footprint. Accessed September 2021.

[43] Jung woo Lee and M. Jae Moon, 'Coming Age of Digital Automation: Backgrounds and Prospects', *Transformation of Work in Asia Pacific in the 21st Century* (2018), pp. 11–56.

ways. Nearly every job is becoming more digital and being transformed in one way or another. And hybrid and remote work is here to stay.

Hybrid and Remote Work

Before the coronavirus pandemic, only 5 per cent of employees worked from home. By May 2020, that number had shot up to 65 per cent.[44] Contrary to prevailing perceptions, productivity levels have remained stable or improved by about 5 per cent with remote work.[45] Perhaps the increase in productivity is due in part to the elimination of daily commutes, which has created more 'work' time for the employees. While there are economic benefits, such as productivity increase for the organization, a whole host of issues and challenges have also surfaced.

While people feel fortunate to still be employed, the collapse of work–life boundaries and the fear of being under constant surveillance of employers have driven people to work harder for longer. With furloughs and the need to pivot business to stay afloat, many employees and teams are spread thin, forcing them to take on much more work than they would under normal circumstances. A study by Workplace Intelligence and Oracle

---

[44] Chandni Kazi and Claire Hastwell, 'Remote Work Productivity Study Finds Surprising Reality: 2-Year Analysis', Great Place to Work, 10 February 2021. Available at: https://www.greatplacetowork.com/resources/blog/remote-work-productivity-study-finds-surprising-reality-2-year-study. Accessed July 2021.

[45] Enda Curran, 'Work From Home to Lift Productivity by 5% in Post-Pandemic U.S.', *Bloomberg*, 22 April 2021. Available at: https://www.bloomberg.com/news/articles/2021-04-22/yes-working-from-home-makes-you-more-productive-study-finds. Accessed July 2021.

showed that seven out of ten employees work on the weekend on a regular basis.[46]

Employees are also experiencing an increased meeting load and a lot more informal communication that digital technologies have enabled. The number of instant messages has markedly increased.[47] Work communication now spreads over a longer workday as employees fall back on different tools to stay connected yet remain productive.

The diminishing boundaries between work and life have led to increased levels of burnout.[48] These are the reasons why productivity and work–life balance have become the top two issues on employees' minds.[49] With the co-location and convergence of work and life, there are a lot of distractions and challenges for employees to deal with. The phrase 'I am tired'[50] is frequently heard. It is found that tiredness is driven by the cognitive overload from working at home and factors such as

---

[46] Dan Schawbel, 'The Balancing Act: What We've Learned from One Year of Working from Home', World Economic Forum, 23 April 2021, available at: https://www.weforum.org/agenda/2021/04/working-from-home-what-we-learned/. Accessed July 2021.

[47] Jaime Teevan, Brent Hecht, and Sonia Jaffe, 'The New Future of Work: Research from Microsoft on the Impact of the Pandemic on Work Practices' (First edn.), Microsoft, 2021, available at: https://aka.ms/newfutureofwork. Microsoft. Accessed July 2021.

[48] Bobbi Thomason, 'Help Your Team Beat WFH Burnout', *Harvard Business Review*, 26 January 2021, https://hbr.org/2021/01/help-your-team-beat-wfh-burnout. Accessed July 2021.

[49] Josh Bersin, 'Remote Work Has Arrived, But It's Not Quite As Great As We Hoped', Joshbersin.com, 10 January 2021, available at: https://joshbersin.com/2021/01/remote-work-has-arrived-but-its-not-as-great-as-we-hoped/. Accessed July 2021.

[50] 'MetLife's 18th Annual US Employee Benefit Trends Study 2020', MetLife, 2021, available at: https://www.metlife.com/employee-benefit-trends/ebts2020-holistic-well-being-drives-workforce-success/. Accessed July 2021.

poor work location, children and pets and other distractions, such as noise from neighbours. Those who are juggling work and have caring responsibilities for children and the elderly, are believed to be struggling the most. A large meta-analysis research study showed that one in three adults, particularly women and those in the lower socio-economic status, are experiencing psychological distress, including high stress levels that have affected their productivity and ability to focus.[51]

Apart from the mental toll brought on by the new norms of work, data from the Pew Research Centre[52] showed that younger workers, especially those who are below fifty years of age, have a much harder time adapting to remote work. They are also less motivated, less able to meet and connect with peers, and less productive.[53]

This is further compounded by the fact that video meetings increase stress levels as measured by brainwave markers because the mental effort required for video meetings is a lot higher than face-to-face meetings.[54] Constant staring at the computer

[51] Maryah Ulpah, Hanifa Maher Denny, and Siswi Jayanti, 'Studi Tentang Faktor Individu, Lingkungan Kerja Komputer dan Keluhan Computer Vision Syndrome (CVS) pada Pengguna Komputer di Perusahaan Perakitan Mobil', *Jurnal Kesehatan Masyarakat*, 3 (3) (2017), pp. 513–523.

[52] John Seabrook, 'Has the Pandemic Transformed the Office Forever?', *The New Yorker*, 25 January 2021, available at: https://www.newyorker.com/magazine/2021/02/01/has-the-pandemic-transformed-the-office-forever. Accessed September 2021.

[53] Kim Parker, Juliana Menasce Horowitz, and Rachel Minkin, 'How the Coronavirus Outbreak Has – and Hasn't – Changed the Way Americans Work', Pew Research Centre, 9 December 2020. Available at: https://www.pewresearch.org/social-trends/2020/12/09/how-the-coronavirus-outbreak-has-and-hasnt-changed-the-way-americans-work/. Accessed July 2021.

[54] Jaime Teevan, Brent Hecht and Sonia Jaffe, 'The New Future of Work: Research from Microsoft on the Impact of the Pandemic on Work Practices', Microsoft, 2021, available at: https://aka.ms/newfutureofwork.Microsoft. Accessed July 2021.

screen is exhausting. Our eyes have a harder time focusing on characters on a computer screen. Unlike print, computer characters are brightest at the centre and diminish towards the edges of the screen. When we want to focus, our eyes 'jump around', thus, making them tired.[55]

Also, a lot more effort is required for employees to actively participate in video meetings as the compression technology that is used and the size of the screen of personal computers reduce non-verbal cues that inhibit one's ability to 'read people'. The pressure of sustained attention and paying attention to others, low media quality, and the fact that crowded remote meetings require cognitive multitasking, all add to the stress levels and fatigue that result from video meetings.

Working remotely can be lonely and isolating, especially for new hires and those who are not in the 'inner circle'. Being glued to the computer screen all day long, meeting colleagues virtually, is not the same as being in the same room, having a cup of coffee or having a chat by the water-cooler. As Satya Nadella, CEO of Microsoft once said: 'digital technology should not be a substitute for human connection'.[56] In research conducted more than a decade before the pandemic, about remote work among journalists, it was found that telework increased loneliness over office work by a whopping 67 percentage points.[57]

---

[55] Ibid.

[56] Yeli Wang , Monica Palanichamy Kala , Tazeen H. Jafar , 'Factors Associated with Psychological Distress During the Coronavirus Disease 2019 (COVID-19) Pandemic on the Predominantly General Population: A Systematic Review and Meta-analysis', *PLOS ONE*, December 2020, available at: https://doi.org/10.1371/journal.pone.0244630. Accessed September 2021.

[57] Sandi Mann and Lynn Holdsworth, 'The Psychological Impact of Teleworking: Stress, Emotions and Health', *New Technology, Work and Employment*, 2 October 2003, available at: https://doi.org/10.1111/1468-005X.00121. Accessed September 2021.

Adapting to Hybrid and Remote Work

Given that many employees are still adjusting to hybrid and remote work, how can organizations address the issues of remote work, yet create a culture and an environment for employees to thrive and be successful and productive in?

The shift to hybrid and remote work is not just about technology and giving employees tools to do their work, it's also about supporting them at the personal and emotional levels. And as we have mentioned in Chapter 1, one of the areas of focus for this is employee experience.

At SAP, the Employee Engagement team frequently organizes several activities every month for employees to promote physical, mental and social health. For example, weekly sessions over Zoom or Teams are held to promote mindfulness and run fitness and well-being classes on Hatha Yoga and UFit. Initiatives such as 'Stay Sane Under Roof' to help employees define physical, mental and emotional boundaries and practise self-care have been rolled out. Sessions for the children of SAP employees, such as coding workshops, have also been offered so employees can get a break from their children while the organization trains the next generation of workers.[58]

Another example comes from Finastra—a corporate payment company. The company rolled out entertaining virtual sessions such as bingo, cooking and arts and craft for the children of their employees—again to give parents employed by the company a break from their children.[59]

---

[58] According to Jovina Ang, who consulted for SAP from 2017 to 2020.

[59] Sharon Doherty, 'Building An Inclusive And Remote Culture', *Forbes*, 3 August 2020, available at: https://www.forbes.com/sites/forbeshumanresourcescouncil/2020/08/03/building-an-inclusive-and-remote-culture/?sh=6d7a8bad279b. Accessed September 2021.

Helping employees cope better also requires organizations to create a culture that promotes camaraderie. As Julian Lute, strategic advisor to the Great Place to Work commented, 'Camaraderie is like a secret weapon. When employees experience the nexus of great work, a powerful mission and shared values, productivity soars.'[60] Camaraderie is critical for building a sense of belonging. Surveys have shown that hybrid and remote work can affect employees' sense of belonging.[61] This issue affects diverse employees and new employees more, as they have not yet established strong social and personal ties. Which is why regular communication and innovative ways to engage employees and create camaraderie are critical to address this important need in Maslow's Hierarchy of Needs.[62] As human beings, we are hardwired for connection and we all have a need for belonging, to feel and be a part of a group or something collective.

Many leaders have started introducing new kinds of meetings and other collaborative practices that have attempted to make up for the loss of face-to-face and the full range of social interaction people had previously relied on at work. Recognizing the power of showing care and personal connection, many leaders have started to establish informal check-ins and talks.

During the lockdown in New Zealand, Rachel Taulelei, CEO of Maori Food and Koon, organized live streams and

---

[60] Chandni Kazi and Claire Hastwell, 'Remote Work Productivity Study Finds Surprising Reality: 2-Year Analysis', Great Place to Work, 10 February 2021, available at: https://www.greatplacetowork.com/resources/blog/remote-work-productivity-study-finds-surprising-reality-2-year-study, accessed July 2021.
[61] 'Report: Remote Work in the Age of COVID-19', Slack, 21 April 2020, available at: https://slack.com/intl/en-sg/blog/collaboration/report-remote-work-during-coronavirus. Accessed September 2021.
[62] Maslow, 'Maslow's Hierarchy of Needs'.

water-cooler talks several times a week for her employees to connect with her. Without a set agenda, employees could dial in via Zoom to talk about dogs, baking and whatever else was on their minds.[63] In doing so, Taulelei was able to build strong professional and personal relationships with her employees. She also created a safe space and provided psychological safety for her employees to voice their concerns, issues or anything that concerned them, while also helping them to cope with the lockdown.

While virtual team bonding is still relatively new, Atlassian, a company that has been practising 'Team Anywhere',[64] a policy that allows its 5,700 employees across the world to work from any location where Atlassian has a corporate entity. The company recently released its 'Team Playbook'[65] on the internet to share some innovative ways to work better together. Similar to running effective meetings, running successful 'plays' incorporates the following steps: (i) doing the preparatory work, (ii) running the play, (iii) leaving with a plan. Furthermore, the company makes a deliberate effort to connect with its remote employees. Activities such as running fun ice-breaking virtual activities and fun remote team activities regularly, helps foster employee connections and friendships in the virtual environment.

[63] Jacinda Ardern, 'Conversations Through COVID-19: Rachel Taulelei', COVID-19 Podcast Series, Facebook, 25 April 2020, available at: https://www.facebook.com/jacindaardern/videos/conversations-through-covid-19-rachel-taulelei/588816781992136/. Accessed July 2021.

[64] Cara Walters, 'Four Times a Year in the Office: Atlassian Goes All in on WFH', *The Sydney Morning Herald*, 29 April 2021, available at: https://www.smh.com.au/business/small-business/four-times-a-year-in-the-office-atlassian-goes-all-in-on-wfh-20210428-p57n4w.html. Accessed July 2021.

[65] Atlassian, 'Atlassian Team Playbook: Building Strong Teams with Plays', 2021, available at: https://www.atlassian.com/team-playbook. Accessed September 2021.

Increased Use of Employee Data

Employee tracking has become a more common practice during the COVID-19 pandemic. Other than tracking infection rates among employees, many companies in Singapore are tracking employees working on-site and remotely. For example, OCBC Bank uses its internally developed app HIP (HR in your Pocket) for these tracking purposes.[66]

Given the time taken to conduct and draw insights from the annual employee engagement surveys, many organizations have started to conduct pulse surveys on a more regular basis, using tools like Qualtrics, Microsoft Forms and Survey Monkey. In general, we observe organizations conducting the pulse surveys every quarter—which are mini engagement surveys—in addition to the annual employee engagement surveys. At SUTD, the results of the quarterly pulse survey have helped the leaders of the university to develop follow-up initiatives to address the issues of employee well-being, stress levels and safety.

Organizations are also starting to increase monitoring of employees. A study by *Gartner*[67] showed that 80 percent of organizations are using non-traditional tools and technology more frequently to monitor their employees using methods such as virtual clocking in and out, tracking work computer usage and monitoring employee emails or internal communications and chats.

There are many digital tools available for employee monitoring. Common communication tools such as Zoom and

---

[66] Interview with Jacinta Low, Senior Vice President of Human Resources, OCBC Bank, 23 March 2021, via Zoom.
[67] Brian Kropp, 'The Future of Employee Monitoring', *Gartner*, 3 May 2019, available at: https://www.gartner.com/smarterwithgartner/the-future-of-employee- monitoring/. Accessed July 2021.

Microsoft Office365 also have a basic monitoring functionality to track employee engagement, well-being and safety. These digital tools can enable stealth monitoring, live video feeds, keyboard tracking, optical character recognition, keystroke recording, or location tracking easily. Other organizations have gone one step further by analyzing big data collected from emails, social media, biometric data, as well as scrutinizing which employees are present in what meetings, and understanding how employees are utilizing their personal workspaces.

The monitoring of employees is a fine line that separates corporate surveillance from employee privacy. There was an uproar in November 2020 when a report about 'bossware' or more specifically, the monitoring capability of Microsoft Office365,[68] was made public. The report showed that managers can measure email activity and the use of shared documents, and how often employees are connecting to the company network, right down to data about the individual worker, data like the number of emails sent, how often they collaborated with other workers and so on.

It is for this reason that managers, particularly Human Resources (HR) leaders need to weigh in on the ethics of monitoring employee data, as well as follow best practices for ensuring responsible use of employee information and data analytics. If not done with trust and openness, such monitoring of employee data can have adverse effects on employee sentiment and well-being, as some employees have reported issues of their perceived inability of switching off from work. This is why organizations need to ensure transparency and full disclosure if they are monitoring the employees.

---

[68] Alex Hern, 'Microsoft Productivity Score Feature Criticised as Workplace Surveillance', *The Guardian*, 24 November 2020, available at: https://www. theguardian.com/technology/2020/nov/26/microsoft-productivity-score-feature-criticised-workplace-surveillance. Accessed July 2021.

Increased Number of Contingent Employees

The prevailing economic uncertainty has led many organizations to move towards hiring more contingent employees as this hiring strategy reduces the fixed cost of hiring and treats the cost of contingent employees as a variable cost. As a cost measure, 80 per cent more companies are expanding their use of contingent workers and 32 per cent of companies are replacing full-time employees with contingent employees.[69] The number of freelance and contingent job openings have also increased by over 25 per cent in the period April–June 2020, compared to January–March 2021.[70]

Much of the demand for contingent employees have come from healthcare institutions, governments, businesses and media organizations. These employees were hired primarily to 'interpret, analyze and report' data on COVID-19 cases, hospitalizations, mortality rates, testing, as well as the impact of the pandemic, which showed the demand for people with mathematical and algorithm-related skills.[71]

The use of more contingent workers provides more flexibility in manpower planning and agility for organizations to respond to change in this disruptive environment. Hiring contingent workers can help plug talent shortages, allow organizations to meet seasonal demands or even gain specialist

[69] Mary Baker, '9 Future of Work Trends Post-COVID-19', *Gartner*, 8 June 2020, available at: https://www.gartner.com/smarterwithgartner/9-future-of-work-trends-post-covid-19/. Accessed July 2021.

[70] Karen Gilchrist, 'The Pandemic has Boosted Freelance Work—and Hiring for These Jobs is Booming', *CNBC Make It*, 6 July 2020, available at: https://www.cnbc.com/2020/07/07/freelance-work-grows-amid-covid-19-math-stats-game-hiring-in-demand.html. Accessed July 2021.

[71] Gilchrist, 'The Pandemic has Boosted Freelance Work'.

expertise as and when the need arises. Even Microsoft has 50,000 contingent workers that are not on their payroll, working in tandem with the 120,000 full-time employees.[72]

However, there are drawbacks to hiring contingent workers. The drawbacks include a lack of commitment, high turnover and security risks. Compared to full-time employees, contingent workers are often perceived not to be as committed to their employing organization due to the temporary nature of their employment contract. Turnover is reported to be higher for contingent workers. And there might be security risks as the screening process is likely not to be as thorough for them, compared to the screening for hiring full-time employees.

Thus, there are management challenges, of which one of the biggest challenges is assimilating these employees into the culture of the organization. Having employed contingent employees in the past, one important step is to make these employees a part of the team. As leaders of organizations, we have both spent considerable time building inclusive organizations to ensure that both full-time employees and contingent workers work and collaborate well together.

Adaptability. Adaptability. Adaptability.

Change and digital disruptions will continue to sweep across all industries and affect every industry and sector, and how businesses are run. If there is one word to sum up what is critical for the modern organization to navigate in a world of

---

[72] 'How the Pandemic Changed Talent Management for the Better', Episode 817, HBR *Ideacast with Johnny C. Taylor Jr.* [podcast], *Harvard Business Review*, 31 August 2021, available at: https://hbr.org/podcast/2021/08/how-the-pandemic-changed-talent-management. Accessed September 2021.

new norms, it is adaptability. Adaptability is no longer a choice but an imperative for the modern organization.

Adaptability towards the new norm of work requires new models of work to be devised. As high as 80 per cent of CEOs believe that their existing business models would be obsolete in the future.[73] Which is why organizations need agile and adaptable business models for them to flex and get to where the opportunities are.

An organization that is highly adaptable is Spotify. Even though Spotify is less than twenty years old, it is now the largest and most popular audio streaming subscription service in the world, with an estimated 365 million users.[74] A key part of Spotify's success is due to the company's unique approach to organizing teams.

The Spotify model of work, which is believed to be the world's best work model for agility, was first introduced by Henrik Kniberg and Anders Ivarsson.[75] It is a model that organizes more around work and less around processes, bureaucracies and hierarchies. It also encourages more self-management and autonomy. And it drives high levels of employee alignment to focus on a common goal, while at the same time, empowers its employees with high levels of autonomy.[76]

---

[73] 'Competing in 2020: Winners and Losers in the Digital Economy', *Harvard Business Review*, 25 April 2017, available at: https://hbr.org/sponsored/2017/04/competing-in-2020-winners-and-losers-in-the-digital-economy. Accessed July 2021.

[74] Spotify Company Info, available at: https://newsroom.spotify.com/company-info/. Accessed September 2021.

[75] Spotify Training & Development, 'Spotify Engineering Culture—Part 1' [video], 3:05 to 4:12, 2013, available at: https://vimeo.com/85490944. Accessed September 2021.

[76] Ibid.

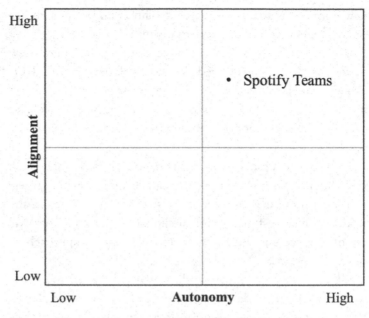

Figure 2.1: Spotify Work Model for Teams
Source: Adapted from Spotify Training & Development, 2013.[77]

Another example of an organization that is designed for adaptability and fluidity is SUTD. From the outset, SUTD was designed to have a fluid structure with no boundaries. The concept of no boundaries and fluidity can be observed in the design of the new SUTD campus that was completed in December 2014. A large proportion of the campus real estate was designed to encourage collaboration and teamwork. Instead of clearly defined floors or spaces for the five different pillars or disciplines that the university specialises in, the seating

---

[77] Adapted from Spotify Training & Development, 2013, 'Spotify Engineering Culture—Part 1' [video], 3:05 to 4:12, available at: https://vimeo.com/85490944. Accessed September 2021.

arrangement encourages teams from different disciplines to be located together.

Whenever there is a new project, resources will be drawn from the different pillars to form a team to provide diverse perspectives. As an example, the electric car project team included individuals with specializations in Humanities, AI, Engineering, Computer Science and Data Analytics, thus, enabling the team to design an electric car design that does not only have autonomous and self-driving capabilities, but also functionalities to sense the environment to move safely with minimal human intervention.

Managerial Implications

Given that hybrid and remote work are here to stay, we would like to recommend the following for effective management of the modern organization:

- Create a sense of belonging by organizing informal, fun and personal activities for leaders to connect with their employees.
- Conduct regular pulse surveys. *Gartner* has recommended the following questions:
  - Do you believe the organization has your best interests in mind when making business decisions?
  - Are you satisfied with the way your organization has managed both its business and people during this time?
  - Has your organization maintained adequate communication with all its employees?
  - Have you continued to collaborate with your team during this time?
  - Does your team inspire you to do your best work?

- ○ Does your team help you complete your work?
- ○ Do you have the appropriate amount of information to make correct decisions about your work?
- ○ When something unexpected comes up in your work, do you usually know whom to ask for help?
- ○ Do you have a good understanding of your organization's informal structures and processes?[78]
- Organize for high alignment and high autonomy.

---

[78] Jackie Wiles, '9 Questions That Should Be in Every Employee Engagement Survey', *Gartner*, 22 August 2020, available at: https://www.gartner.com/smarterwithgartner/the-9-questions-that-should-be-in-every-employee-engagement-survey/. Accessed July 2021.

Chapter 3

The Roles of Leaders and Managers

Continuous learning is critical for leaders and managers to stay relevant and be successful. Given the rapid changes in our environment, past successes are not good predictors for future successes.

Work cannot exist without leaders and managers. This is why leadership and management are integral aspects of organizational success. They are not the same thing.

In general, leadership is about inspiring, motivating and innovating, whereas management is about managing the business to a rhythm or the cadence of the business. On the one hand, leaders play an important role in creating the right culture, motivating employees, setting the direction and making the right decisions, based on evidence and data. On the other hand, managers play a role in aligning the organization with a set of goals and metrics. And good managers know how to plan, organize and coordinate. If you want to use one word to differentiate what leaders do and what managers do, you may say that leaders 'inspire' and managers 'manage'.

Leadership and management are popular topics, as shown by the billions of search results on the internet. A search on Google would reveal at least 2.8 billion results for leadership[79] and 4.7 billion results for management[80]. Having worked as a leader and a manager at multiple Fortune 500 companies and taught leadership and management at several universities, I[81] have come to appreciate that different leadership and management styles are needed for different situations and tasks. Similarly, different styles are needed for motivating and inspiring people. I have also learned that an important trait of a good leader and a good manager is to take action. It is better to make a bad decision rather than do nothing at all, as doing something can help to rule out the things that do not work.

The roles and expectations of leaders and managers are getting increasingly complex. There are countless challenges for leaders and managers to address, from industry disruption and evolving technology, to the global pandemic, demographics imbalances and shifting cultural norms and generations. Since the coronavirus pandemic broke out, stress has risen to an all-time high and affected employee well-being in a big way— adding to the list of things that leaders and managers need to look after.

Given that organizations cannot function without leaders and managers, what exactly do they do?

---

[79] Search results as in September 2021.
[80] Search results as in September 2021.
[81] 'I' here refers to Jovina Ang.

What Managers Do

If you ask managers what they do, they will most likely tell you that they plan, organize, command, coordinate and control. These five words have dominated management vocabulary since they were first introduced by Henri Fayol in 1916.[82]

However, these five words merely skim the surface of what managers actually do. To thoroughly understand the roles of managers, Walter Borman and Donald Brush[83] conducted an extensive review of management literature and compiled the many roles of managers. These roles are wide and varied, comprising:

- Planning and organizing
- Guiding, directing and motivating subordinates
- Training, coaching and developing subordinates
- Communicating effectively and keeping others informed
- Representing the organization before customers and the public
- Having the technical proficiency to run a business or perform a function
- Administration and paperwork
- Maintaining good working relationships
- Coordinating with subordinates and other resources to get the job done
- Decision-making and problem solving

---

[82] Patrick Ward, 'Management Theory of Henri Fayol: Summary, Examples', NanoGlobals, 29 August 2021, available at: https://nanoglobals.com/glossary/henri-fayol-management-theory/. Accessed September 2021.
[83] Walter C. Borman, and Donald H. Brush, 'More Progress Toward a Taxonomy of Managerial Performance Requirements', *Human Performance 6*, no. 1 (1993), pp. 1–21.

- Staffing
- Persisting to reach goals
- Handling crisis
- Driving organizational commitment
- Monitoring and controlling resources
- Delegating
- Selling/influencing
- Collecting and interpreting data

Even though planning and organizing rank high on the list of things that managers do, in most research studies, on a day-to-day basis, managers do not demonstrate that they are systematic planners.[84]

Furthermore, in an in-depth study that involved observation as a method of research, Henry Mintzberg[85] found that managers typically work at an unrelenting pace. Their activities are characterized by brevity, variety and discontinuity. They are oriented towards action. And they dislike reflective activities. For example, it was found that more than 50 per cent of CEOs' tasks and activities last less than nine minutes. And only one in 368 activities that CEOs do involves some sort of general planning.

What Leaders Do

To understand what leaders do, we thought it was important to look at the literature on leadership.

The topic of leadership has been studied since the 1800s, which is why there are many theories of leadership.

---

[84] Ibid.
[85] Henry Mintzberg, 'The Manager's Job: Forklore and Fact', *Harvard Business Review*, March–April 1990, available at: https://hbr.org/1990/03/the-managers-job-folklore-and-fact. Accessed September 2021.

However, the most researched and referenced theories of leadership are the 'transactional leadership' and 'transformational leadership' theories. These theories of leadership were first introduced by James MacGregor Burns[86] and subsequently refined by Bernard Bass.[87]

Leadership is transactional when a leader influences others with what they offer in exchange, similar to what you would do in a transaction or an exchange. Transactional leadership involves making contingent rewards and punishment, in response to action or inaction from the employees. This leadership style is centred on getting results and being in control. Whereas transformational leadership revolves around a leader's influence on his or her employees. Transformational leadership is centred on winning the hearts and minds of employees; trust is a key component of this leadership style.

According to Bernard Bass, there are four components or four I's that provide the basis for transformational leadership. These include:

- *Idealised influence*: This 'I' refers to the leader's charisma, self-confidence, determination, power, capabilities, ethical standards and values, which enable them to influence and persuade.
- *Inspirational motivation*: This is all about how a transformational leader uses symbols, artifacts, emotional appeal and enthusiasm to help employees envision attractive future states. A transformational

---

[86] James MacGregor Burns, *Leadership* (New York: Harper and Row, 1978), pp. 141–400.
[87] Bernard M. Bass and Ronald E. Riggio, *Transformational Leadership* (New Jersey: Lawrence Erlbaum Associates, Inc., 2006).

leader often crafts vision to inspire and motivate employees

- *Intellectual stimulation*: A transformational leader would challenge employees to think by asking questions to stimulate innovative and creative solutions. At times, a transformational leader might even reframe problems to encourage employees to look at a problem from a different perspective.

- *Individualised consideration*: Given that employees have different needs, a transformational leader would take the employee's own consideration into account when he or she is developing the employee. The leader might incorporate mentoring, two-way exchanges and good delegation.[88]

Another key characteristic of transformational leaders is they see themselves as change agents. They are risk-takers and they possess exceptional cognitive skills and believe in careful deliberation before taking action.

As shown above, it is evident that transactional leadership and transformational leadership are distinctly different leadership styles. In a meta-analysis research study, Timothy Judge and Ronald Piccolo found that both of these styles are effective in driving outcomes for the organization.[89] What this suggests is that different leadership styles are required for different situations or contexts. In other words, leadership is situational and contextual.

---

[88] Ibid.

[89] Timothy A. Judge and Ronald F. Piccolo, 'Transformational and Transactional Leadership: A Meta-Analytic Test of Their Relative Validity', *Journal of Applied Psychology*, 89, no. 5, 2004, pp. 755–768.

Furthermore, successful leadership in the past cannot guarantee success in the future. As Bill Gates once said, 'Success is a lousy teacher. It seduces smart people into thinking they can't lose.'[90]

Even Fortune 500 companies are not 'immune' to failures, as shown by the high failure rate: 88 per cent of Fortune 500 companies that existed in 1955 no longer exist today.[91]

The Delusion of Success

Why do companies, especially successful companies, fail? The list of failures is long and getting longer. Think Kodak. Digital Equipment Corporation. Robinsons. Once successful companies in their heydays, they are now either shadows of their former selves or no longer exist.

Company failures are not only a phenomenon of the West. Even Singapore companies are not immune. Robinsons, the once popular retailer that every woman in Singapore counted on, ceased its 162-year operations and shut its doors in 2021. Many Singapore women lamented the demise of Robinsons—it was the go-to store for them to find the latest fashion, buy the latest kitchen appliances or speak to an auntie[92] for advice.

[90] Jamie Johnson, '10 Bill Gates Quotes Every Business Owner Needs to Hear', *CO* by U.S. Chamber of Commerce, 10 January 2020, available at: https://www.uschamber.com/co/start/strategy/bill-gates-business-quotes. Accessed September 2021.

[91] Mark J. Perry, 'Fortune 500 Firms in 1955 vs. 2014; 88% are Gone, and We're All Better off Because of that Dynamic "Creative Destruction"', *AEIdeas*, 18 August 2014, available at: https://www.aei.org/carpe-diem/fortune-500-firms-in-1955-vs-2014-89-are-gone-and-were-all-better-off-because-of-that-dynamic-creative-destruction/. Accessed September 2021.

[92] 'Auntie' is a term used as a sign of respect for an older lady in Singapore and Malaysia.

One reason why successful companies fail is due to the delusion of success. The delusion of success can mire down successful companies to think that nothing could possibly go wrong for them. Often, these companies have been found to have clung too tightly to the strategy that had propelled them to greatness.

Kodak's downfall was not because of technology. Kodak was so blinded by the success of its film business that it completely missed the rise of digital technologies, even though the first prototype of a digital camera was created by Steven Sasson in 1975,[93] a young engineer who worked for Kodak. The film business model had become so entrenched in its strategy that CEO after CEO at Kodak ignored the shifting trend towards digital photography and missed the opportunity to be the first company to move into this product category.

Digital Equipment Corporation (DEC), the company that invented the mini-computer, also fell prey to the delusion of success. At the height of its success, DEC was a colossus of the computing industry. It dominated mini-computers the same way Microsoft is dominating personal computers today. When it ignored the trends towards personal computers and open source, it lost its foothold as a powerhouse in the IT industry.

The delusion of success is not an issue that only affects companies in technology. The demise of Robinsons, Singapore's flagship departmental store, can be attributed to the company's resistance to change. Robinsons clung too tightly to its traditional retail business model, while its competitors were quick to jump onto the e-retailing bandwagon.

Organizational failures are not a phenomenon of the past or a result of the coronavirus pandemic. In fact, organizational

---

[93] James Estrin, 'Kodak's First Digital Moment', *The New York Times*, 12 August 2015, available at: https://lens.blogs.nytimes.com/2015/08/12/kodaks-first-digital-moment/. Accessed September 2021.

failures are becoming common today. The lifespan of companies is also getting shorter. The average lifespan of companies is between fifteen and twenty years today, compared to thirty and thirty-five years in 1970.[94]

The coronavirus pandemic also had a huge toll on businesses across the world. Since the start of the pandemic, over 30 per cent of small businesses have shut down, whether you look at the statistics in the United States[95] or Singapore[96], due to factors including economic contraction and reduced trade flows within the country or across the local region, and the world.

Continuous Learning

Leadership is a craft that must be continuously learned in order to stay ahead and survive in this period of unprecedented change. According to Michael Useem, 'There's no medication to make you a leader, no pill you can take, no simple solution for it. It's often a lifelong process.'[97]

[94] S. Patrick Viguerie, Ned Calder and Brian Hindo, '2021 Corporate Longevity Forecast', *Innosight*, May 2021, available at: https://www.innosight.com/insight/creative-destruction/. Accessed August 2021.
[95] Chris Nichols, 'Fact-check: Have One-third of US Small Businesses Closed during Pandemic?', *Austin American-Statesman*, 8 June 2021, available at: https://www.statesman.com/story/news/politics/politifact/2021/06/08/kamala-harris-small-business-closures-covid-fact-check/7602531002/. Accessed September 2021.
[96] 'The Big Read: COVID-19 Decimated Their Promising Business, but Some Entrepreneurs aren't Afraid to Try Again', *Channel News Asia*, 26 April 2021, available at: https://www.channelnewsasia.com/singapore/big-read-covid-19-decimated-their-promising-business-some-entrepreneurs-arent-afraid-try-again-241866. Accessed September 2021.
[97] 'Learning to Be a Better Leader', Knowledge@Wharton, 20 July 2021, available at: https://knowledge.wharton.upenn.edu/article/learning-to-be-a-better-leader/. Accessed September 2021.

The way leaders lead tomorrow will be very different from how they lead today. The core skills of leaders are long-term vision, strategy building, sound decision-making, persuasive communication and an understanding of how everything around them is changing, whether it's the way work is being conducted today, shifts in customer needs or changes in the demographics of their workforce.

Hence, a leader's job in a radically changing world is to stand on the cliff edge, get a grip on unfamiliar landscapes, and acquire the skills for leading the enterprise into new territory. Every leader needs to find the edge for leaping across the breach and breaking new ground on the other side.

In Michael Useem's latest book, *The Edge: How 10 CEOs Learned to Lead—And the Lessons for Us All*,[98] he profiled ten leaders in their learning journey of transforming their respective organizations. Each of the ten leaders took different paths.

Given the trend towards digital technologies, Mark Turner, former chairman of WSFS Financial Corporation, spent three months on the road visiting forty-nine companies, from Apple to Walmart. He wanted to get to the roots to understand how technology is changing consumer behaviour and how it would affect and revolutionize the banking industry. With the insights from his 'listening tour', he restructured the bank to offer fintech services on top of traditional banking services.

Another leader featured in the book is William Lauder of The Estée Lauder Companies. As a company, Estée Lauder was dependent on the cosmetics counters in departmental stores. And since the inception of the company, Estée Lauder had focused its promotional strategy on providing cosmetic samples

---

[98] Michael Useem, *The Edge: How Ten CEOs Learned to Lead—And the Lessons for Us All* (London: Hachette, 2021).

to new and existing customers. Given the pervasiveness of digital technologies and the rise of China, he wanted to make Estée Lauder more nimble, and going online was one strategy to adopt. But the culture of doing things as they were done was deeply entrenched in the company. In order to drive change, he approached Fabrizio Freda of Procter & Gamble to ask him to become his COO. Freda subsequently became CEO, when Lauder assumed the role of Executive Chairman. Both the leaders worked as partners. This was an unusual combination, with the Executive Chair and the CEO joined at the hip to make changes, make waves and turn the place upside-down, in order to culturally redirect a change in strategy for developing alternative business models for the company.

While it took a decade to make the change, the majority of the company's sales no longer come from the departmental stores' cosmetics counters, and its promotional strategy goes well beyond providing cosmetic samples to customers.

Anthro-vision

Besides being open to change, learning to lead is also about adopting 'anthro-vision'[99]. Anthro-vision, which is looking at things from the eyes of an anthropologist, is particularly useful for solving business problems. As Gillian Tett, the author of *Anthro-vision* said, 'Every business problem is a human problem. And every human problem and every data point represents some human behaviour at its core.'[100]

---

[99] Gillian Tett, *Anthro-Vision: A New Way to See in Business and Life* (New York: Simon and Schuster, 2021).
[100] Ibid.

Adopting anthro-vision can help us understand ourselves, our tribes, companies and communities, and reduce our wilful blindness and unconscious bias. Anthropological insights are not derived from surveys or empirical research, but from fieldwork—from directly observing and talking to people. It is observing what people do, noticing the rituals that are important for people, but also observing what people don't do. In so doing, leaders can learn more about the 'why'—the reason for things happening—and not only the 'what'. This perspective is something that scientific data or big data cannot tell us. Also, big data only works when it is put into a built model. Big data might not work when the situation or context changes.

There are three principles that all leaders can learn from anthropologists to widen our thinking and approach to solving business problems. The three principles are:[101]

- *Make the strange familiar*
  As human beings, we often shy away from cultures and people that seem 'strange' to us. Anthro-vision offers the chance to embrace the strange and the associated culture shock. A method such as ethnography, which is essentially spending time listening and observing, can reveal insights into why people do what they do.
  For example, when Nestlé found that the teenagers were giving each other Kit Kats as lucky charms for exams, the company reinvented its marketing strategy to focus on lucky charms as the penetration strategy for entering the Japanese market.

---

[101] Ibid.

- *Make the familiar strange*

  There is a Chinese proverb that says that a fish can't see water. Which suggests that it is very hard for us to see ourselves unless we step out of ourselves and look back afresh.

  The 2008 Global Financial Crisis was one of the worst economic disasters in this century which nearly triggered the collapse of the banking system. One of the main causes of the crisis was driven by the sub-prime mortgage situation. However, the situation went undetected because banks were bundling the sub-prime mortgages with prime mortgages. This example suggests that it is important to step 'outside' and look back to avert any future crisis, even though things might appear to be going well.

- *Listen to social silence as what people do (actions) speak louder than what they say (words)*

  As human beings, we are prone to lazy assumptions and unconscious biases as we are products of our social, cultural and physical patterns.

  We use models, scorecards, key performance indicators (KPIs) and balance sheets to navigate the world of work, and lead. There are limitations to the tools that we use. These models, scorecards and so on are limited, as they are as good as the data that is used to measure them.

  For example, the corporate balance sheet is not the way to measure the success of a company. Other factors, including diversity and inclusion, environmental, social and governance (ESG) goals also matter for determining the health of a company.

Importance of Culture

Another important role of leaders is to build an optimal culture for the organization. Culture is so important that Peter Drucker, the late management guru allegedly said, 'culture eats strategy for breakfast'. To elaborate further,

> 'Strategy is on paper, whereas culture determines how things get done. Anyone can come up with a fancy strategy, but it's much harder to build a winning culture. Moreover, a brilliant strategy without a great culture is "all hat and no cattle", while a company with a winning culture can succeed even if its strategy is mediocre. Plus, it's much easier to change strategy than culture.'[102]

Hence, it is easy to see why culture is the secret sauce that keeps employees motivated and customers happy. Culture also has enormous influence over how employees show up at work, how they interact with each other, how they conduct business transactions and how they deal with customers.

As discussed in Chapter 1, culture, which is essentially the DNA of the organization, is the factor that brings an organization together and aligns its workforce to a common mission and values to achieve a common goal and key business objectives.

If culture is so fundamental to an organization's success, how do leaders get culture right?

To answer this question, let us look at Microsoft's culture transformation journey. It is probably one of the best examples of

---

[102] Ken Favaro, 'Strategy or Culture: Which Is More Important?', *Strategy+Business*, 22 May 2014, available at: https://www.strategy-business.com/blog/Strategy-or-Culture-Which-Is-More-Important. Accessed September 2021.

getting culture right in the world. Since becoming CEO in 2014, Satya Nadella transformed the once siloed, hard-to-partner-with company into one which embraced collaboration and cooperation across the ecosystem of partners. Since Nadella's appointment as CEO, Microsoft's market capitalisation has grown from US$381.7 billion in 2014 to US$2.3 trillion in 2021.[103]

Growth Mindset

In speaking to my[104] former colleagues at Microsoft, I was told by many of them that at the heart of Microsoft's culture transformation is how Nadella was able to bring about a mindset shift from a 'fixed mindset' to a 'growth mindset'.

Before we expand on the definitions of fixed mindset and growth mindset, allow us to explain what a mindset is. A mindset is a way of thinking. It can determine whether we succeed or fail at something. It can also influence what we can accomplish, how we do things and the risks we take.

Carol Dweck, the researcher who first discovered the 'power' of the growth mindset, defines it as a mindset that is forward-looking and open to learning.[105] The growth mindset is not constrained by boundaries. It does not assume that people are limited by a lack of ability or are born with a set level of intelligence. Rather, people with the growth mindset tend to try new things, take measurable risks and are not constrained by the fear of failure.

---

[103] Companies Market Capitalisation, 'Market Capitalisation of Microsoft (MSFT)', 2021, available at: https://companiesmarketcap.com/microsoft/marketcap/. Accessed September 2021.

[104] 'My' in this instance refers to Jovina Ang's.

[105] Carol S. Dweck, *Mindset: The New Psychology of Success*, (New York: Random House, 2008).

In contrast, a fixed mindset is a mindset that is firm, unchanging and static in nature. People with fixed mindsets have the belief that they are limited by the talents or intelligence that they are born with, and that they cannot get smarter no matter how hard they try.

The growth mindset has cultivated a deep sense of purpose within every Microsoftie.[106] It has also challenged every employee to answer questions such as 'Why am I here?'[107] and 'How can I make a difference to the world?'[108]

The culture transformation of Microsoft was a 'test and learn' approach that relied heavily on the use of data to monitor, as well as take corrective actions, to go from the current culture to creating an aspiring culture.

As explained by Kathleen Hogan, Microsoft's Chief People Officer:[109]

> 'Being open about failure helps us balance a growth mindset with accountability. We are learning to not just reward success, but also reward people who fell short while getting us closer. We don't need people to show up in meetings having memorized pages of information to look smart. We want it to be perfectly acceptable to say, "I don't have that

---

[106] 'Microsoftie' is an informal term for Microsoft's employees.

[107] Peter Cohan, 'Culture Is The Most Surprising Reason Microsoft Stock Will Keep Rising', *Forbes*, 30 January 2020, available at: https://www.forbes.com/sites/petercohan/2020/01/30/culture-is-the-most-surprising-reason-microsoft-stock-will-keep-rising/?sh=159daca41b23. Accessed September 2021.

[108] Satya Nadella, Greg Shaw and Jill Tracie Nichols, *Hit Refresh: The Quest to Rediscover Microsoft's Soul and Imagine a Better Future for Everyone* (London: HarperCollins, 2017), p.101.

[109] Ibid.

information, but I can get it." Learning from our mistakes gets us closer to our desired results—that's a new form of accountability for us. That's the journey.'

Furthermore, research conducted by Microsoft showed that employees with the growth mindset do far more than develop innovative products and solutions. The growth mindset also drives employees to collaborate and work together for the success of the company.

To inculcate the growth mindset, Microsoft embeds the growth mindset curriculum in its learning and development strategy. For example, Microsoft now organizes annual hackathons[110] during the One Week celebration, for employees to step outside their day jobs to develop leadership skills such as collaborating across disciplines and advocating for ideas. Any employee who has an idea or a hack that has business and societal merit is encouraged to share that idea and solicit support from people across the whole organization to join their team. Additionally, the newly formed team is tasked to develop the business plan, create the prototype, and pitch it to the executive team. If the executive team sees potential in the project, funding is given to build the project and take it to market.

Other than hackathons, teams across Microsoft can also participate in high-risk projects, which are peripheral projects that are not core to the company's business. As an example, 'Project HoloLens', a project that is based on holographic

---

[110] Carol Dweck and Kathleen Hogan, 'How Microsoft Uses a Growth Mindset to Develop Leaders', *Harvard Business Review*, 7 October 2016, available at: https://hbr.org/2016/10/how-microsoft-uses-a-growth-mindset-to-develop- leaders. Accessed September 2021.

computing,[111] is in the high-risk category. Project HoloLens offers a visual computing platform controlled by speech and gesture that is intuitive and provides one the unique capability to interact with other human beings, environments or objects.

Microsoft's new talent development programme,[112] which is centred on the principles of the growth mindset, assumes that every Microsoftie has potential to lead and grow. Which explains why Satya Nadella and his executive team meet with the heads of each business unit on a yearly basis to review their employees and brainstorm methods to augment skills and build experiences.

A growth mindset is fundamental for learning and growth at both the individual and organizational levels. Microsoft recommends the following strategies:[113]

- Hire people who embrace challenges and like to collaborate
- Attract people who want to improve
- Encourage positivity
- Lead by example with flexibility at the top
- Do not punish failure
- Encourage team development that focuses on increasing positive outcomes and innovation
- Be forward-thinking by looking at the big picture.

---

[111] Jessi Hempel, 'Microsoft in the Age of Satya Nadella', *Wired*, February 2015, available at: https://www.wired.com/2015/01/microsoft-nadella/. Accessed September 2021.

[112] Carol Dweck and Kathleen Hogan, 'How Microsoft Uses a Growth Mindset to Develop Leaders', *Harvard Business Review*, 7 October 2016, available at: https://hbr.org/2016/10/how-microsoft-uses-a-growth-mindset-to-develop-leaders. Accessed September 2021.

[113] Microsoft 365 Team, 'Grow Your Business with a Growth Mindset', Microsoft, 12 June 2020, available at: https://www.microsoft.com/en-us/microsoft-365/business-insights-ideas/resources/grow-your-business-with-a-growth-mindset. Accessed September 2021.

Developing and Inspiring People

'Before you are a leader, success is all about growing yourself. When you become a leader, success is all about growing others.'[114]

There are many lessons that we can learn from Jack Welch, whom many still believe is the best leader at developing people to ever have lived. In his years at General Electric (GE), it is believed that Jack Welch spent half his time getting the right people in the right places and helping them thrive. He also avoided the typical practice of assigning the most promising leaders to the larger businesses to manage. Instead, he often sent his star performers to places where GE had a small presence so they could learn and grow.

From the time he joined GE, Welch was obsessive about the values of transparency and honesty. He did not mince his words. And he spoke with candour and gave frank feedback to help his people continually grow and develop.

He was also obsessive about 'pumping up his people' and instilling confidence in them. He once quipped, 'One of the jobs you have as a manager is to pump everyday self-confidence into your team to make them feel great, to make people like me feel like I've got a full head of hair and I'm 6'10"'.[115]

While you might think that cheerleading is an odd role for a leader, it has, on the contrary, become an important part of leadership during the pandemic, which saw soaring stress levels

---

[114] Jack Welch, Suzy Welch, Bodo Primus, Helmut Winkelmann, Susanne Grawe and Marian Szymczyk, *Winning* (New York: HarperCollins, 2005).

[115] Thomas Koulopoulos, '5 Unforgettable Leadership Lessons From "Manager of the Century" Jack Welch', *Inc*, 2 March 2020, available at: https://www.inc.com/thomas-koulopoulos/jack-welch-ceo-general-electric-business-leadership-management-lessons.html. Accessed September 2021.

and increasing incidences of mental health issues. A leader who is a cheerleader tends to do the following four things well:[116]

- They focus on the employee's strengths
- They empathize
- They give recognition
- They create psychological safety

Finally, if there was one leadership philosophy that we can all learn from Jack Welch, it is to 'love 'em to death'. He has been reported to say:

'Get the hell out of the office. Get out and touch the people. Listen, listen, listen. Love 'em to death and touch them, get inside their skin. Excite them about what they're doing. Give purpose to their jobs and their lives. That's what this is all about. We spend most of our waking hours on these jobs. Make them fun, make them exciting, and reward the hell out of the ones who do the job you ask them to do.'[117]

Managerial Implications

Given how past successes are not a good predictor for future successes, as leaders and managers, it is imperative to ask yourself the following questions to stay ahead of the curve:

---

[116] Stephanie Vozza, 'Six Habits Of People Who Know How To Bring Out The Best In Others', *Fast Company*, 1 May 2016, available at: https://www.fastcompany.com/3054826/six-habits-of-people-who-know-how-to-bring-out-the-best-in-othersm. Accessed September 2021.

[117] Thomas Koulopoulos, '5 Unforgettable Leadership Lessons From "Manager of the Century" Jack Welch', Inc, 2 March 2020, available at: https://www.inc.com/thomas-koulopoulos/jack-welch-ceo-general-electricbusiness-leadership-management-lessons.html.

- Am I continuously learning to lead?
- In order to solve problems better:
  - How do I make the strange familiar?
  - How do I make the familiar strange?
  - How do I listen to social silence?
- How can I create an optimal culture that is centred on the growth mindset?
  - Do I organize events or activities that allow people to put forth their ideas?
  - How do I transform the learning and development strategy to develop my employees' potential?
  - How can I create an environment that encourages collaboration right-to-left and top-to-bottom in the organization?

Chapter 4

Data is the New Oil

Clive Humby once said: 'Data is the new oil.'[118] *But to ensure that data is truly the new oil, we need to make sense of it. The process of making sense of data requires careful planning, research and most importantly, combining it with empathy and behavioural science, so that the right insights can be drawn for effective decision-making and managerial action.*

Leaders and managers need to work with data alongside managing culture change and transformation. We are living at the precipice of major transformations being brought on by technology in the world today. In the book *Mega Tech: Technology in 2050*, Daniel Franklin discussed the radical innovations in technology in areas such as medicine, law, automotives, transportation, construction, farming and agriculture.[119]

---

[118] Ritu Janager, 'Data is the New Oil', The Commerce Society, 10 June 2021, available at: https://comsocsrcc.com/data-is-the-new-oil/. Accessed September 2021.

[119] Daniel Franklin, *Mega Tech: Technology in 2050*.

One of the most impactful areas driving radical innovations is big data analysis. Big data is data that is large, fast and complex, and is usually difficult or impossible to process using traditional methods. It can contain structured and unstructured data from many sources, and these include data streamed from social media, smart devices, transactions, audio and video files and email logs, amongst many others. These data sets can be mined for information and used in machine learning projects through predictive modelling and other advanced analytics applications.

Also, AI, mobiles, social media and the Internet of Things (IoT) are driving data complexity through new forms and sources of data. The analysis of this extensive set of data allows data analysts, researchers and business users to make faster and better decisions that previously were not possible. Today, data is flowing through mobile networks at a faster rate than ever before. In the 2021 *Ericsson Mobility Report*,[120] it was found that mobile data traffic around the world had hit 49 exabytes (10^{18}) a month by the end of 2020 and had topped 66 exabytes a month in the first quarter of 2021. Ericsson predicts that by 2026, mobile data traffic will hit a total of 237 exabytes a month.

Kimberly Miltz[121] of Statista reported that the global big data and business analytics market was valued at US$168.8 billion in 2018 and is forecast to grow to US$215.7 billion from 2021. In addition, the size of the business intelligence and analytics software application market is forecast to reach around US$16.5 billion in 2022.

---

[120] Ericsson, *Ericsson Mobility Report 2021*, June 2021, available at: https://www.ericsson.com/4a03c2/assets/local/mobility-report/documents/2021/june-2021-ericsson-mobility-report.pdf. Accessed October 2021

[121] Kimberly Mlitz, 'Big Data and Business Analytics Revenue Worldwide 2015–2022', Statista, available at: https://www.statista.com/statistics/551501/worldwide-big-data-business-analytics-revenue/. Accessed October 2021.

The growth of this market is driven by a focus on digital transformation, data visualization and increased adoption of cloud computing. Without a doubt, big data is radically transforming organizations and industries through the power of advanced analysis and tools to provide deep insights for planning business and marketing strategies.

Nations are also going digital. Forward-looking governments, such as Singapore, are fast transforming themselves into smart nations through the use of big data. In an article about the Singapore Government's vision for the Future Economy, it was reported that Minister Chan Chun Sing remarked that 'data is a valuable economic resource that allows Singapore to overcome its intrinsic limitations on land, human capital and natural resources'. During the transformation process, the country is also empowering its citizens to access data, as well as encouraging companies in the private sector to play a key role in driving business innovations through big data.

One example of big data application in Singapore refers to the key collection process of the Housing and Development Board (HDB) flats. HDB worked with GovTech, an all-government technology agency, to analyze over 90,000 emails to garner feedback on the key collection process, which led to the development of an online form for new homeowners to book an online appointment to collect the keys to their new flats, leading to greater efficiency and user satisfaction.[122]

Many other innovations in big data analysis have and will continue to revolutionize every industry and sector. Even industries such as healthcare and the legal profession have embraced big data analysis. In the near, foreseeable future, diagnosis in the field of medicine will be impacted by computer-aided

---

[122] Ibid.

diagnostic tools. This will lead to improvements in automatic tracking of data, thus diminishing the role of doctors. In the legal profession, it is predicted that advanced algorithms will have the ability to review court documents faster than humans, thus enabling fairer judgement and outcomes, and removing human cognitive biases.

The rapid transition from computer science to real-world scenarios means that there will be:

- Reduced amount of data to be processed by human beings
- Better compression of data
- Early detection of irrelevant data
- More effective sampling methods

As more data becomes available, it will enable us to detect patterns that are far more subtle.[123] This has three implications for work: first, things that are hard to do today will become easier. Second, things that are costly to do today will become cheaper. And third, things that are scarce today will become more abundant.

On the sustainability front, instruments called macroscopes can collect and organize data from billions of connected devices to help us better understand our world and manage climate change and address the triple bottom line measures.[124] These solutions use geospatial data like climate and soil conditions, and other data such as social and political conditions of a country, to provide insights that could help us to solve issues of global food

---

[123] Kenneth Cukier, 'The data-driven world' in *Mega Tech: Technology in 2050*.
[124] Triple Bottom Line or TBL refers to measures pertaining to profits, people and planet.

shortages and other environmental challenges, such as climate change and global warming.

All these technological advancements will lead to an innovation economy where information and data are the new currency, and talent and ideas the new forms of organizational capital. This means that AI, data science and 3D printing will be some of the new skills that are already needed now, and will continue to be in the future.

Furthermore, anyone can reskill and upskill today. With widespread connectivity across the world, anyone can have access to digital networks to acquire knowledge, communicate with one another, and conduct businesses—a thing that was not possible several years ago. All these innovations allow ordinary people to learn and upgrade themselves continuously.

In the article 'Preparing for Digital as the New Normal', Juergen Reiner discussed:

> 'As the world becomes ever more connected—the number of Internet of Things (IoT) devices is expected to increase by 250 per cent by 2020, to more than 8 billion—and with new technologies finding their way into industrial operations, a "new normal" is emerging. The new business environment will be dominated by ecosystems that will enable multiple producers and business-to-business (B2B) customers to connect.'[125]

Which is why in this new age of rapid digital transformation, data-driven skills will be the key to success, coupled with expert

---

[125] Juergen Reiner, 'Preparing for Digital as the New Normal', *Oliver Wyman*, November 2017, p.2, available at: https://www.oliverwyman.com/content/dam/oliver-wyman/v2/publications/2017/nov/Preparing-for-digital-as-the-new-normal.pdf. Accessed September 2021.

analysis and the ability to understand data analytics and make sense of mountains of data. The use of prescriptive analytics to extract insights for scenario planning and decision modelling is currently being employed in many industries, especially in logistics, aviation, banking, healthcare, manufacturing and so on.

As technology becomes more sophisticated and machines become smarter and better able to learn and evolve by themselves through a process called machine learning, more sophisticated learning neural models will evolve. These models will help businesses make use of data to improve customer engagement, conduct businesses on the internet and operationalize the many management processes needed to effectively run an organization.

Kiran Bhageshpur[126] in his article 'Data is the new oil' opined that data is the new oil as its applications do not just serve business purposes, but also have great value in saving lives and managing sustainability. Data collection through aircrafts and drones can help governments and agencies analyze the data to manage evacuations during natural disasters. Other examples include machine learning systems that have the ability to detect breast cancers more accurately than human pathologists. The future of automotives lies with the use of autonomous vehicles that are powered by data. These vehicles will result in more efficiency; it is predicted that the number of cars on the road will reduce by up to 75 per cent, resulting in massive reductions in greenhouse gas emissions (GHG).[127]

---

[126] Kiran Bhageshpur, 'Data is the New Oil and That's a Good Thing', *Forbes*, 15 November 2019, available at: https://www.forbes.com/sites/forbestechcouncil/2019/11/15/data-is-the-new-oil-and-thats-a-good-thing/?sh=3d22a6d17304. Accessed October 2021.
[127] Ibid.

The many examples and case studies show that data is here to stay. Thus, organisations will not have a choice but to embrace and develop a data culture, as well as the discipline for using data analytics effectively. And we believe that data discipline needs to be driven by leaders and inculcated by managers.

Kevin Buehler and Nicolaus Henke reinforced this important point by describing data as follows:

> 'Data is a double-edged sword. It's fueling new business models and transforming how companies organize, operate, manage talent, and create value. It also poses risks: data-security questions, privacy concerns, and uncertainty about ethical boundaries are unavoidable. For leaders, the ability to seize the potential of advanced analytics, while simultaneously avoiding its hazards, is becoming mission critical.'[128]

Additionally, data that is used should not be confined to the usual operational data (O data) such as employee tenure, revenue and profit margin. There is a trend that is leaning towards experience data (X data). Turning experience data into unforgettable service can help build long-lasting emotional connections with the customer. Which is why X data will be the most potent resource for organizations. The more customized the service, the more personalized the care and the more intimate the engagement, the more satisfied the customer will be. Both types of data are paramount to business success. This is why any organization's

---

[128] Alejandro Díaz, Kayvaun Rowshankish, and Tamim Saleh. 'Why data culture matters'. *McKinsey Quarterly*, No. 3, 2018, available at: https://www.mckinsey.com/~/media/mckinsey/business%20functions/mckinsey%20analytics/our%20insights/mckinsey%20quarterly%202018%20number%203%20overview%20and%20full%20issue/mckinsey-quarterly-2018-number-3.ashx. Accessed September 2021.

comprehensive data strategy needs to incorporate X and O data, as well as big data.

Developing a Data Strategy

Before embarking on building a data strategy for your organization, it is important to be clear about your overall business strategy and your key business questions. Only when you understand what you are trying to solve does data become effective for decision-making.

Hence, it is important to identify at least three (or a maximum of four) key imperatives so that you can focus on the projects that can yield the most promising results for your organization. In order to have some quick wins, we recommend that you focus on the 'low-hanging fruit' that have the most impact.

In my experience of working for a large security organization, I[129] started with a data project that impacted the recruitment of security manpower to address an accelerated manpower need of the customer. This simple project resulted in the company winning multi-million dollar manpower contracts in building key infrastructures across Singapore.

When you have identified the key business area and priorities, the next step is to determine the data requirements. This is a fundamental step for you to accurately consolidate data from the various sources, as well as empower employees across the multiple business functions to produce insights for decision-making and action. As you go through this journey, you might have to make several refinements, which is why it is called the 'customer journey refinement'.

---

[129] 'I' refers to Jaclyn Lee here.

Nick Ismail[130] recommended moving away from a silo mentality, as an increasing amount of data would be collected by every single team, department and business. The full cycle of data and information—from creation to governance and compliance, archival, and finally, disposal—must be carefully managed across the entire organization to keep it under control. Data would also need to be broken down into X and O data.

X data can be integrated with the strategies to drive customer loyalty, leadership trust index and so on. This data can also be visualized in dashboards to review the hidden patterns and trends, for decision-making. X data can also be derived from advances in technology, through tools such as sentiment analysis and big data analysis to improve customer or employee experience. Whereas O data is data that can help leaders and managers run their organizations better and meet their KPIs.

These are the reasons why it is important to establish a data selection strategy at the outset. In so doing, the chances of biased outcomes in data science are reduced. Data can be sourced from 'everywhere'. By which, we mean:

- Multiple systems and company databases
- Legacy documents
- Traditional media
- Social media
- Apps
- Cloud
- Web

---

[130] Nick Ismail, 'From Just Visible to Truly Valuable: How to Manage Big Data in the Age of Digital', *Information Age*, 13 January 2017, available at: https://www.information-age.com/how-manage-big-data-digital-age-123463978/. Accessed October 2021.

- Internet of Things
- Social networks
- Social influencers
- All user activities including typing on the keyboard, a swipe of the phone—all can generate data
- Data warehouse appliances
- Network and in-stream monitoring technologies
- Surveys including both from quantitative and qualitative surveys

Given the extent of sources available for organizations to obtain data, it is imperative that the parameters for ensuring data quality, security, privacy, ownership, as well as ethics, are defined for data use.

Technology considerations are important when developing your data strategy. This includes having the right technology and infrastructure to collect, store, process and communicate the data. Lastly, it is important to ensure that the workforce has the right data skills and knowledge to extract meaning from data for effective decision-making.

The data culture that you are trying to inculcate has to be driven top-down. Other than promoting a data culture, as a leader of your organization, it is important that you ensure that there is data literacy across the entire organization for an effective enterprise-wide data strategy implementation.

Application of Data in Talent Management

One of the key applications of data is in the area of talent management. Today, organizations are beginning to realize that the ability to use data to provide insights for managing the workforce gives them a competitive advantage in their businesses.

Google, which is the third most valuable firm in the world, has cited people analytics as one of the major reasons for its success. Its extraordinary people management practices have resulted from its use of people analytics. Because of its data capability, Google has been able to make accurate, data-based people management decisions[131], and this has had a great impact on its success as a company that has rolled out many innovations in search and communication and productivity tools.

Many years ago, Google established a strong people analytics team that uses data to drive fact- or evidence-based decision-making in almost all aspects of human resource management. Some examples of its best practices include how Google has been able to accurately identify the top eight characteristics of successful leaders in a project called 'Project Oxygen'. Project Oxygen uses Google's PiLab to analyze effective approaches for maintaining a productive environment. It also uses a retention algorithm to predict employee turnover, and there is also a predictive model for workforce planning. What is amazing about this is the ability it has endowed Google with, to calculate the value of its top performers. For example, Google has been able to determine that the performance differential between an exceptional technologist and an average employee is 300 times.[132]

Additionally, in this post-pandemic world, human capital has become central to and the core of organizational success.

---

[131] Emily Grace, 'How Google is using people analytics to completely reinvent HR', PeopleHum, 10 August 2020, available at: https://www.peoplehum.com/blog/how-google-is-using-people-analytics-to-completely-reinvent-hr. Accessed September 2021.

[132] Ibid.

Due to the rapid digitalization fuelled by the pandemic, there has been a huge demand for talent and skills; this demand is only expected to accelerate. Furthermore, given the pervasiveness of technology and the need to use digital tools for collaboration, talent is now boundaryless. 'The global talent pool has arrived, and talent is the new global currency . . . *if* businesses have the culture, confidence, and technology to tap into it.'[133]

During this challenging time, it has become more crucial to improve ways of efficient management and utilization of people resources. Given that one of the most critical and challenging parts of crisis management is prioritization,[134] people analytics will help leaders gain insights for decision-making, while having the ability to examine the demographics and location data to identify high-risk employees. The data will also provide an understanding of the recent pandemic developments and initiatives for organizations to integrate public health dashboards with the people analytics systems.

Organizations with people analytics capabilities have many competitive advantages compared to those that are still using anecdotal information to make key people decisions.[135]

---

[133] Becky Frankiewicz and Tomas Chamorro-Premuzic, 'The Post-Pandemic -Rules of Talent Management', *Harvard Business Review*, 13 October 2020, available at: https://hbr.org/2020/10/the-post-pandemic-rules-of-talent-management. Accessed September 2021.

[134] Ivana Kotorchevikj, 'The Role of People Analytics in Managing the COVID-19 Crisis in the Organization', *Towards Data Science*, 31 August 2020, available at: https://towardsdatascience.com/the-role-of-people-analytics-in-managing-the-covid-19-crisis-in-the-organization-8d25070569b. Accessed October 2021.

[135] Elizabeth Ledet, Keith McNulty, Daniel Morales and Marissa Shandell, 'How to be Great at People Analytics', McKinsey, 2 October 2020, available at: https://www.mckinsey.com/business-functions/organization/our-insights/how-to-be-great-at-people-analytics. Accessed September 2021.

For example, there exists a large global organization that is using the key elements of the data science process to create a homegrown weekly pulse survey to track the opinions and feelings of tens of thousands of its globally dispersed employees. Through the survey, many issues including mental health were detected. Insights such as these are critical for organizations to understand what the better ways to support their employees are, especially those who are mainly working remotely.

What is People Analytics?

The competitive advantages of people analytics are plenty, but what exactly is people analytics? It is the systematic identification and quantification of the people drivers that drive business outcomes to enable better decision-making and ultimately, improve the business return on investment (ROI). Evidence-based human resources practices that are based on data, can elevate the HR function from good to great. The impact of the issues of human and cognitive biases and subjectivity can also be reduced. And people analytics can help to answer commonly asked questions such as:

- Will our managers become more effective if they go for leadership training?
- Is our current performance measurement system effective?
- Are we hiring the right talents?
- How effective are our recruitment processes?

When leaders and managers have the ability to measure the effects of their intervention more accurately in talent lifecycle, rewards, performance management, as well as employee experience, it can help them to better address issues resulting from mergers and acquisitions, divestments, strategic workforce planning, cost management and critical talent issues and so on. Hence, as shown in the Venn diagram below, people analytics is a function that sits in the intersection of business strategy, math/statistics, and systems. (Figure 4.1).

Strategy is key for people analytics to work. It is absolutely fundamental to understand the business problem, including why data is needed at the first step. Fermin Diez, Mark Bussin and Venessa Lee, in their book on the fundamentals of HR analytics, said:

> 'It is important to have an understanding of the business as the basis of framing questions. With a strong understanding of how the business works, you will be able to understand the context and ask the right questions . . . Be sure to obtain

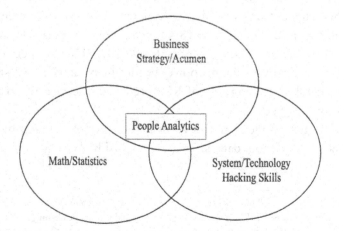

Figure 4.1: Venn Diagram of People Analytics

Source: Author's own

agreement on the business issue the analytics project will address.'[136]

The science of people analytics is centred on the scientific method, research and survey design, as well as the experimental design. The systems component refers to data management and warehousing, and the organization's visualization tools. The statistics component refers to the tools and techniques used to analyze data such as correlation, multiple linear regression, logistic regression, mathematical models and machine learning.

DBS Bank's 'Project Marvel'[137] shows how the bank has used people analytics to drive performance for its relationship managers (RM). By examining the data, determining the good attributes of a high-performing RM and the factors driving early RM attrition, the bank was able to develop a predictive index tool for smarter hiring of RMs, as well as provide the necessary sales coaching for the RMs who were falling short of their targets. Consequently, the bank was able to reduce attrition rates from 27 per cent to 18 per cent, while at the same time, saving costs amounting to S$170,000 (~ US$126,000) per year. To better plan for its manpower needs, the bank went one step further by providing a list of RMs predicted to leave early, to the bank managers.

Data is indeed the new oil in the modern organization. Having a strong data strategy, along with the right culture,

---

[136] Fermin Diez, Mark Bussin and Venessa Lee, *Fundamentals of HR Analytics: A Manual on Becoming HR Analytical* (Bingley: Emerald Group Publishing, 2019).

[137] 'Project Marvel' [video], YouTube, posted by DBS, 21 February 2017, available at: https://www.youtube.com/watch?v=IjOH4eHSlSY. Accessed October 2021.

talent and systems to drive data adoption, will provide organizations and even nations with competitive advantage in today's digital world.

Managerial Implications

How do you get started with developing a data strategy? You can start by reviewing the following suggestions and steps:

- Conduct a deep dive with your senior team to review the key business challenges and how data can support you in providing insights into these areas.
- Start with the business problem for which you already have access to the necessary data. If not, develop a simple tool or survey instrument to collect that information.
- Assemble a data team that combines the expertise of technologists, data scientists, subject-matter experts and visualizers.
- Work with your team to draw a strategic business map, such as the balance scorecard to identify key competitive strategies for your organization.
- Develop four to five key HR imperatives to support the process quadrant. These key imperatives will become use cases for you to start the people analytics journey.

Chapter 5

Setting up a Data Analytics Organization

Setting up a data-driven organization requires courage, boldness and dedicated leadership for it to succeed.

In the previous chapter, we built upon the importance of the use of data in organizations and of having a clear data strategy. The starting point for building a data analytics function requires leaders to assemble a multidisciplinary team with the right skills and talent to support the data imperatives. As the data journey takes form, the strongest data teams will evolve with time, based on factors such as culture, strategy, business model and maturity.

In an article entitled 'Building an Effective Analytics Organization', Gloria Macias-Lizaso shared: [138]

---

[138] Gloria Macías-Lizaso Miranda, 'Building an Effective Analytics Organization', McKinsey, 18 October 2018, available at: https://www.mckinsey.com/industries/financial-services/our-insights/building-an-effective-analytics-organization. Accessed September 2021.

'Top-performing organizations in AA [Advanced Analytics] are enabled by deep functional expertise, strategic partnerships, and a clear centre of gravity for organizing analytics talent. These companies' organizations usually include an ecosystem of partners that enables access to data and technology and fosters the co-development of analytics capabilities, as well as the breadth and depth of talent required for a robust program of AA.'

Hence, the ability to build and develop the analytics expertise while investing in the right platforms and technology for extracting data will be key to a successful analytics programme. Going beyond that, it is critical for all the members of the organization to have basic data and computational skills so that everyone in the organization is adept at using data.

In my[139] experience working in both the private and public sectors, I have been involved in data science projects in the areas of workforce planning as well as predictive analytics. In these projects, I have found that having a senior sponsor to support and work alongside myself was the key factor driving the success of the projects.

This insight is aligned with the views of Carl Carande, Paul Lipinski and Traci Gusher: [140]

'Leadership teams must recognize that being successful will take courage, because once they embark on the journey, the insights from data analytics will often point to the need for

---

[139] 'My' and 'I' refer to Jaclyn Lee here.
[140] Carl Carande, Paul Lipinski and Traci Gusher, 'How to Integrate Data and Analytics into Every Part of Your Organization', *Harvard Business Review*, 23 June 2017, available at: https://hbr.org/2017/06/how-to-integrate-data-and-analytics-into-every-part-of-your-organization. Accessed September 2021.

decisions that could require a course correction. Leaders
need to be honest with themselves about their willingness to
incorporate the insights into their decision making, and hold
themselves and their teams accountable for doing so.'

Another important factor to consider is the alignment of the
organizational culture with the organizational structure. A data-
driven culture can bring a multitude of benefits for the business,
including better decision-making. And an organization that has
successfully built a data-driven culture is likely to have teams
that are inclined to seek out and use data in every facet of their
work. The teams are also more eager to take on an active role in
measurement and analysis.

That said, in the journey of becoming more computational,
organizations will face multiple roadblocks. In a *Gartner* survey
of 291 respondents on what they thought were the most critical
roadblocks to building successful data teams, respondents
answered that the top three roadblocks were culture challenges,
lack of resources, and poor data literacy. The report also
highlighted that data and analytics is not a technology
implementation, rather it is a change management initiative.[141]

Practical Ways to Start the Analytics Journey

How do organizations start their data journey? An important
advice from the team at McKinsey[142] is to start with the existing

---

[141] Laurence Goasduff, 'Avoid 5 Pitfalls When Building Data and Analytics
Teams', *Gartner*, 9 July 2020, available at: https://www.gartner.com/
smarterwithgartner/avoid-5-pitfalls-when-building-data-and-analytics-teams.
Accessed October 2021.

[142] Charles Atkins, Mitra Mahdavian, Katelyn McCarthy and Michael Viertier,
'Starting the Analytics Journey: Where You Can Find Sales Growth Right

data that your organization has access to. These suggesions include:[143]

1. Start with existing high-quality data and metrics, while laying the foundation for consistent data collection;
2. Use high-quality data and metrics to dynamically generate insights and inform speedy decision-making;
3. Use advanced analytics and machine learning to predict outcomes and automatically trigger events.

Beginning the data journey with existing data already available within your organization can help you tap into the potential of low-hanging fruit.

The Data Science Cycle

Before we tell you more about how to set up a data analytics organization, let us first indulge in giving you an overview of the data science cycle. Understanding this cycle can provide crucial guidance if you are unfamiliar with how the journey goes. It also gives you a framework to work with data. This cycle consists of six separate and linked steps. While we have illustrated the steps with reference to setting up a people analytics function, the steps equally apply to other functions, for example, setting up a marketing analytics operation.

Now', McKinsey, 18 April 2018, available at: https://www.mckinsey.com/business-functions/marketing-and-sales/our-insights/starting-the-analytics-journey. Accessed September 2021.
[143] Ibid.

Step 1: Asking the Right Questions

Some examples of business questions that you can ask include the following:

- What is the most critical business issue faced by your managers?
- What are the main people-related challenges that affect your company's ability to execute on corporate goals and strategies?

Step 2: Selecting the Right Data

As data is an indispensable asset for organizations, an enterprise-wide data strategy is needed to accurately consolidate data from various sources, empower employees across multiple business functions, and produce insights for employee journey refinement. Data that is comprehensive and actionable can help fuel behaviour prediction, enrich employee experience and develop more targeted human resource programmes. Which is why it is important to establish a data selection strategy prior to collecting data, to decrease the chance of a biased outcome in data science.

Step 3: Data Collection

Data collection is an important part of your data strategy because it can help to supplement and enhance existing data. There are multiple ways for organizations to collect data, such as:

- Surveys
- Online tracking
- Transactional data tracking

- Online marketing analytics
- Social media monitoring
- Subscription and registration data
- In-store traffic monitoring.

Step 4: Data Cleansing

Having quality data is fundamental to the data science process. Old and inaccurate data can have an impact on results. Data cleaning or cleansing is the process of ensuring that your data is correct, consistent and usable. This process includes identifying any errors or corruption in data, correcting or deleting the data while manually processing it and making system adjustments so that the errors can be prevented in the future. Most of the time spent in data science is consumed by this step. There are many types of data cleaning tools available in the market that can analyze raw data in bulk and automate the process for you.

Step 5: Data Analysis

The fifth step in the data science cycle is data analysis. There are altogether four levels of data analysis, starting from descriptive analytics to prescriptive analytics. The four levels are described briefly as follows:

1. <u>Descriptive analytics</u>: Descriptive analytics help to summarise the existing data using the current business intelligence tools to better understand what is going on or what has happened. Most of the organizations today can perform this basic level of data analysis.
2. <u>Diagnostic analytics</u>: Diagnostic analysis is one step beyond descriptive analytics because it can help organizations use past data to answer the 'what' and

'why' behind the things that they are facing. Diagnostics analytics can be displayed in an analytics dashboard.

3. Predictive analytics: At the predictive analytics level, organizations can predict problems using statistical modelling and machine learning techniques. Google's Project Oxygen described in Chapter 4 is an example of predictive analytics.

4. Prescriptive analytics: This advanced level of analytics uses scenario planning and modelling to predict possible outcomes using data.

Step 6: Data Storytelling

The last step in data science cycle is data storytelling. It is a method for delivering messages derived from complex data analysis in a way that allows the audience to quickly and easily assimilate the material, understand the meaning behind the data, and draw conclusions from it.

Data storytelling does not require showing a ton of data. Rather, it is about sharing the data that matters most to the audience in the most appealing way so that the right action can be incited.

Setting up a successful data analytics organization requires focus and dedication in order to extract insights from data. Milind Parikh[144] summarized the six factors that are required for success:

1. Keeping business value and user personas (refers to users whose goals and characteristics represent the needs of a larger group of users)

---

[144] Milind Parikh, 'Critical Success Factors to Setting up a Data and Analytics Organization', LinkedIn Pulse, 9 January 2018, available at: https://www. linkedin.com/pulse/critical-success-factors-setting-up-data-analytics-parikh-cisa-pmp/. Accessed September 2021.

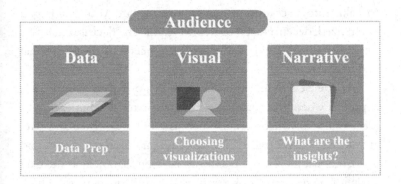

Figure 5.1: Data Storytelling

Source: Authors' own work.

2. Making standard tools, methods and processes available
3. Establishing a horizontal data analytics organization to deliver on the goals
4. Balancing data democratization with proper prioritization, governance, security and traceability
5. Simplify and modernize data discovery, registration, acquisition, integration, curation and consumption
6. Easy access to data through well-built system architectures

The first steps in setting up a data analytics organization requires a functional understanding for picking the right data to solve the most immediate business problems. The systematic use of the data science cycle will facilitate teams to begin the data journey.

Organizing the Data Analytics Team

Team organization is another important decision in the setting up of your data analytics organization. There are many considerations to take into account, of which one is: are you building a centralized, decentralized or hybrid team? The decision that you finally make will be dependent on the needs of the functional and business units.

At the SUTD, the decision was to go with a hybrid team approach where the analytics expertise is embedded in each unit (decentralized), while matters such as data governance and data architecture are centralized. While setting up the function, we had to ensure that there was organizational wide alignment as the data analytics projects we took on were cross-disciplinary in nature. We also sought help from a consultant in the areas where deep analytics expertise was required. These approaches resulted in early wins and successes for SUTD to achieve organizational goals.

There are many models that you can adopt to develop an analytics team. According to Jane Griffin and Tom Davenport,[145] five of these are:

1. *The centralized model:* In this model, a group of analysts would act as a core unit to serve the entire company. The strength of this model is the ability of the team to cross functional boundaries.
2. *The consulting model:* This model works like a consulting organization, where the group of analysts who are located centrally are assigned to projects in the organization and their costs are recovered through transfer pricing.
3. *The centre of the expertise model:* While the analysts are based in the business functions and units, their activities are coordinated by a small centralized group.

---

[145] Jane Griffin, and Tom Davenport, 'Organising Analytics from the Inside Out', Deloitte, 2014, https://www2.deloitte.com/content/dam/Deloitte/us/Documents/deloitte-analytics/us-da-organizing-analytics-inside-out.pdf. Accessed October 2021.

4. *The functional model:* This model places analysts within the specific function that are leading and dominating the analytical activities within the organization. Hence, this model helps to concentrate expertise in areas where there is a high level of need.

5. *The dispersed model.* In this model, the analysts are spread throughout the organization. The drawback of the model is that there exists no mechanism to facilitate collaboration or coordination of efforts.

The choice of the models will depend on the level of analytical maturity and strategy of the organization.

Embarking on the Analytics Journey with People Analytics

As organizations shift towards embracing a more data-driven approach in the different segments of the business, they will soon realize that this approach can help them become more effective in decision-making while elevating the capability for developing strategy.

As mentioned in the previous chapter, people analytics is an area that is gaining a lot of traction in organizations across the world at present. Mike West found that the majority of organizations that have embraced people analytics have either increased efficiency or used analytics to answer new questions that have emerged.[146]

As mentioned in Chapter 4, there are two types of data that are required. The O data is typically extracted for efficiency-oriented projects and they are obtained from HR Information Systems (HRIS). This data is typically cleansed and transformed before it is transferred to the data warehouse for the analysts to publish it on self-service dashboards for timely reporting.

---

[146] Ibid.

The X data or the experience data is typically extracted from insights-oriented projects. In these projects, often a business question is formulated before a hypothesis is developed for experimentation and observation.

Efficiency-Oriented Projects

Efficiency-oriented projects require organizations to align their people strategy with their business strategy so that the right targets can be chosen for measurement. The 'balanced scorecard'[147] measures the health or the efficiency of an organization using four perspectives or quadrants. These include:

1. The financial perspective (earnings per share, return on total assets, return on equity, etc.)
2. The customer perspective (market share, customer satisfaction, brand recognition, customer retention, customer complaints, etc.)
3. The internal business process perspective (cycle time, cost of services, capacity usage rate, labour utilization rate, etc.)
4. The learning and innovation perspective (employee productivity, employee satisfaction, number of cross-trained employees, leadership development, etc.)

To illustrate how these four perspectives come together, let us refer to an example from an IT solutions company (Figure 5.2) with a vision 'to be a leading-edge solutions provider and foremost systems integrator in South Asia'.

---

[147] Robert S. Kaplan, and David Norton, 'The Balanced Scorecard: Measures that Drive Performance', *Harvard Business Review*, 70 (1), January–February 1992, pp. 71–79.

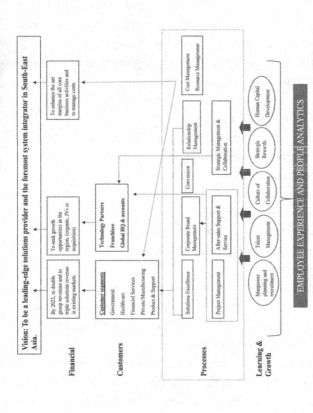

Figure 5.2: IT Solutions Company Balanced Scorecard Efficiency Project

Source: Adapted from Robert S. Kaplan and David P. Norton, *The Balanced Scorecard*.[148]

---

[148] Robert S. Kaplan and David P. Norton, *The Balanced Scorecard—Translating Strategy into Action* (Boston: Harvard Business School Press, 1996).

The company aims to double its financial targets at the group level and triple its solutions revenue in the existing markets. The company also wants to enhance the net margins of all its core business activities, while at the same time, managing costs. In the customer quadrant, the company wants to focus on key customers in the select segments of the industry. It also wants to cultivate the right partnerships with technology providers, franchise owners and the global headquarters.

In the process quadrant, the company has chosen to focus on the following eight factors:

1. Solutions excellence
2. Project management
3. Corporate brand management
4. After-sales support and service
5. Conversion rates of customers
6. Strong relationship management skills
7. Strategic management and collaboration
8. Cost and resource management

In the people quadrant, the company has selected five talent capabilities, including strategic manpower recruitment, talent management, culture of collaboration, competitive total rewards and strategic capability development.

To begin the people analytics process, KPIs were set up to measure the O data to drive the efficiencies of the people processes in the organization. To tell you more, let us illustrate by sharing an example on how to enhance the process for recruitment management. In the strategic quadrant, solutions excellence is a talent capability that is needed to provide superior solutions to its clients. We begin by aligning the resourcing activities so that the best talents with the expertise in

IT solutioning and project management skills can be recruited. Correspondingly, this process is performed while managing costs and reducing time consumed in finding leads to source the appropriate talents.

The next step involves developing measurable KPIs as shown in Figure 5.3.

The type of data is oriented towards improving efficiency (O data). And the data can be tracked using dashboards and HR reports.

Additionally, as we all know, strategic talent management cannot be done in isolation. It is a process that encompasses looking at the employee lifecycle journey map. Figure 5.4 shows the data points that can be used to link the employee lifecycle journey.

Other than what has been described above, there are many other examples of points that may be used to track process efficiencies.

Tracking Resourcing Analytics

There are many types of people analytics measures that can be tracked and monitored. Let us begin with resourcing analytics. These analytics can provide insights for the recruiting teams to improve their hiring process. In determining the effectiveness of recruiting, there are three key metrics that you would want to take note of. These include time-per-status, source-of-hire and referral rates.

- Time-per-status answers the question: How long are you spending on each step of the recruitment process. This simple analytic can make a difference to a recruitment team and help them understand if there are any chokes at each step of the recruitment process. Statistical tools such as Analysis of Variance (ANOVA) can highlight if there are bottlenecks in the recruitment process.

RECRUITMENT					
	HR Deliverables		KPI	Current Score	Target
Strategic	Solutions Excellence		*Top positioning in the sector for solutions excellence	6	Top 3
			*Revenue Size	$100 million	$200 million
Employee Growth	Hire Top Talents		*Percentage of talent with networking and PM capabilities	10 percent	20 percent
Financial	Reduce recruitment cost		$per hire		
Process	Decrease Lead Time	Employer Brand	*Time to hire	50 days	35 days
			*Conversion Rate	50%	70%
			*Employer Brand Index	Top 50%	Top 20%

Figure 5.3: Measuring the KPIs for Elevating Strategic Manpower

Source: Adapted from Erik Van Vulpen, 'The HR Scorecard: A Full Guide'.[149]

---

[149] Erik Van Vulpen, 'The HR Scorecard: A Full Guide', AIHR, available at: https://www.aihr.com/blog/hr-scorecard/ accessed October 2021.

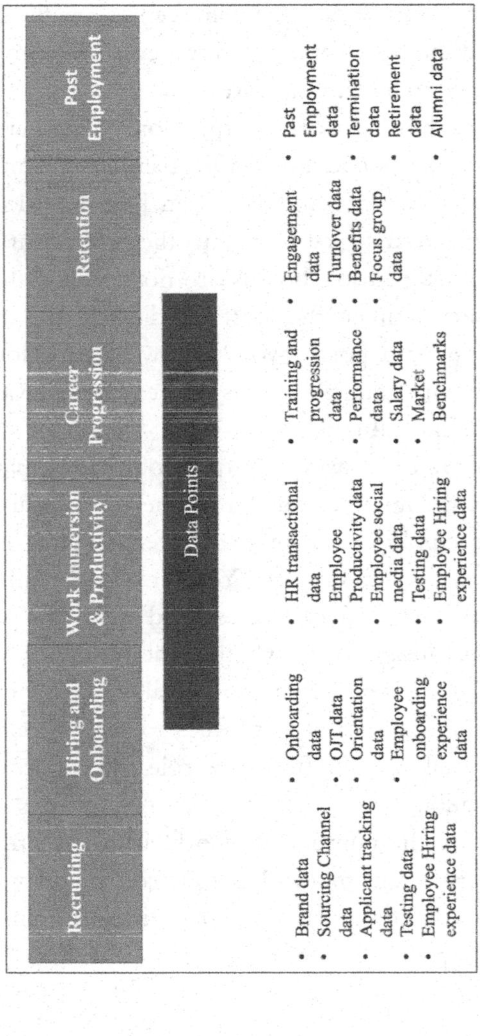

Recruiting	Hiring and Onboarding	Work Immersion & Productivity	Career Progression	Retention	Post Employment
		Data Points			
• Brand data • Sourcing Channel data • Applicant tracking data • Testing data • Employee Hiring experience data	• Onboarding data • OJT data • Orientation data • Employee onboarding experience data	• HR transactional data • Employee Productivity data • Employee social media data • Testing data • Employee Hiring experience data	• Training and progression data • Performance data • Salary data • Market Benchmarks	• Engagement data • Turnover data • Benefits data • Focus group data	• Past Employment data • Termination data • Retirement data • Alumni data

Figure 5.4: Data Points Linking the Employee Lifecycle Journey

Source: Authors' own.

From the ANOVA Figure 5.5, you can see the average number of days taken by each department to hire a candidate, from advertising of the role to signing of the offer letter. Each vertical line represents the sample size and the horizontal line represents the number of days taken to hire a candidate.

- Source-of-hire answers the question: Where are your best candidates coming from? A critical examination of the sources of candidates can help to tailor your recruitment strategy to tap into the best talent pools. If you find that job boards are not yielding the best candidates—rather the best candidates are coming from LinkedIn posts—you may want to tailor your recruitment strategy to focus on generating awareness through LinkedIn instead.

- Referral rates answer the question: How many of your new employees are hired due to referrals from existing employees? Employee referrals often lead to better-quality candidates. Your existing employees know the referred candidates and they can provide additional insight as to whether the candidates would be fit for the vacant role and overall company culture. It is also unlikely for employees to refer a candidate who is unlikely to be fit for the role and culture of the organization.

   If the number of candidates hired through this recruitment method is low, you might want to rethink your organization's incentive programme to ramp it up.

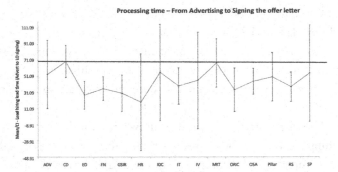

Figure 5.5: Tracking Recruitment Efficiencies using ANOVA Analysis

Source: Authors' own.

Please also refer to Chapter 7 to understand how the OCBC Bank is developing its resourcing analytics.

Learning Analytics

Learning analytics is the measurement, collection, analysis and reporting of data about learners for the purposes of understanding and optimizing learning, as well as tracking the efficiency of the training programmes.

Learning analytics can uncover insights and answer the following questions:

- Which training need is likely to yield the best ROI?
- When is the ideal time to use the different delivery media?
- Which medium or a combination of media is best for the different work groups, e.g. new hires, the sales force, senior leaders?

The Kirkpatrick model, as shown in Figure 5.6, is a well-known and popular model for measuring training effectiveness. Levels 1 to 3 measure and track the efficiency of the programmes, and can be easily completed by looking at the subscription rates and attendance to ascertain the demand for certain learning programmes.

The Kirkpatrick model also allows for the linking of the training strategy to the business strategy to show a line of sight to the impact on the company's bottom line. At Level 4 of the model, leading indicators can be used to bridge the gap between the individual initiatives and efforts, and organizational results. Examples of the leading indicators include job effectiveness, job impact, average change in performance appraisal ratings over time, customer satisfaction ratings, employee engagement scores, turnover, and productivity.

> Level 1: Reaction
> Level 2: Degree which participants acquire
>   the intended knowledge, skills and
>   attitudes based on their participation
> Level 3: Degree participants apply what they
>   learn on the job
> Level 4: Targeted outcomes occur after learning

Figure 5.6: The Kirkpatrick Model of Training Evaluation

Source: Adapted from 'The Kirkpatrick Model'.[150]

---

[150] 'The Kirkpatrick Model', Kirkpatrick Partners, available at: https://www.kirkpatrickpartners.com/Our-Philosophy/The-Kirkpatrick-Model. Accessed October 2021.

Rewards Analytics

Rewards analytics provides insights into the effectiveness of the company's reward strategy. It can also help to answer some of the following questions for better talent management and development:

- Is the reward strategy effective in motivating the best-performing employees?
- What are the critical drivers of employee retention?
- What is the impact of pay, benefits or the environment?
- Is the reward strategy aligned to the changing demographics or generational trends?
- Can the reward strategy identify the critical talent segments in the workforce?

Conducting a correlation analysis among these performance drivers or variables can provide a deeper level of insight (see Figure 5.7).

- *Performance driver analysis:* This is a type of analysis that can help you understand the effect of pay and other rewards on performance. Figure 5.7 below is a sample correlation analysis that shows the relationship between the different performance factors.

The correlation between two different variables can be calculated by a number known as the correlation coefficient (r). The correlation coefficient is a number that ranges from −1 to 1, and it measures the strength of the linear relationship between two variables.

In the example above, you can see that the correlation coefficient 'r' of the factor 'Relationship with current manager'

	Performance Rating 2021	Age	Monthly Income	Relationship with current manager (scale of 1-10)	Number of Sick Leave taken	Number of Annual Leave taken	%increase in sales revenue due to training	Employee Benefits	Job Satisfaction	Years in Company	Years in Current Role
Performance Rating 2016	1										
Age	0.015604452	1									
Monthly Income	-0.00226844	0.493337	1								
Relationship with current manager(scale of 1-10)	0.801107684	0.037863	0.009251	1							
Number of Sick Leaves taken	-0.01344294	0.005767	0.017639	-0.10792	1						
Number of Annual Leaves taken	0.017262045	0.003944	0.017381	0.02116	0.07164	1					
%increase in sales revenue due to training	0.724747429	0.003634	-0.02403	0.60625	-0.02506	0.009726	1				
Employee Benefits	-0.02726813	0.051073	0.013721	0.00865	-0.04969	-0.05361	-0.03672	1			
Job Satisfaction	0.006775048	-0.02149	0.032968	-0.0149	-0.02395	0.077693	-0.00328	0.02475	1		
Years At Company	0.008649453	0.311309	0.509167	0.03818	-0.00461	0.031937	-0.035991	0.019194	0.01208919	1	
Years In Current Role	0.038993751	0.212901	0.361064	0.06191	0.009116	0.020363	-0.00152	-0.014857	0.0498565	0.758754	1
Years Since Last Promotion	0.016300671	0.216544	0.343426	0.04128	-0.02142	0.029792	-0.024959	0.034731	0.01056037	0.616295	0.549901

Figure 5.7: Sample Correlation Analysis of Performance Drivers

Source: Authors' own.

is 0.801107684 (close to 1), which indicates that there is a strong relationship between relationship with manager and performance. The analysis also shows that there is no relationship between pay and performance.

- *Top talent analysis:* As mentioned in Chapter 4, Google's Project Oxygen showed that there is a performance differential between an exceptional technologist and an average one. An exceptional technologist at Google can perform 300 times better than an average technologist.

  The reasons as to why you would want to perform a talent analysis are to answer the following pertinent questions about driving a high-performing team:
  - ° Do you have a view of the employee mix and talents that will drive profitability?
  - ° Are you able to calculate the value of top performers?
- *Turnover driver analysis:* This type of analysis helps you to take a deeper dive into turnover data. You can examine the turnover data and further ask yourself questions such as the following:
  - ° How can you 'slice and dice' data to review the turnover for critical jobs or groups of employees?
  - ° How can you use data analytics to understand employee preferences for the types of benefits or reward structures that are tied to retention?
- *Employee benefits analysis:* In this analysis, data-driven metrics such as engagement measures, attrition, absenteeism and employee surveys are monitored together with benefit take-up rates over time, to ascertain the impact and value of benefits, as well as justify the expenditure for the same. This is illustrated in Figure 5.8.

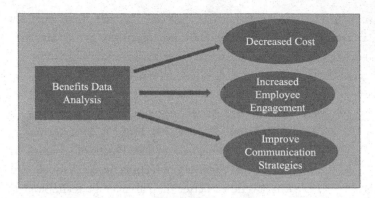

Figure 5.8: Sample Correlation Analysis of Performance Drivers

Source: Authors' own.

- *Competency acquisition analysis:* This analysis informs insights to ascertain the core competencies that are critical for your organization to succeed. Following this step, you could decide if you would like to develop or acquire these competencies through the hiring of new employees. This can be done by taking a talent inventory of your current competencies and comparing it against future competencies that might be needed.

As you can see from these examples, data analytics can be used to address the critical people issues that are important for the business. It is crucial that these issues are addressed as they can hinder the organization's ability to execute on corporate strategies to meet goals. Additionally, analytic techniques can show patterns, trends and correlations between variables to help you design better programmes to drive organizational effectiveness and use its talents, including how to attract, recruit, develop and retain the top talents.

Leveraging X Data

The second type of people analytics data that is important is that of X data that could be used to enhance the function of HR analytics. As mentioned previously, X data is experience data.

- *Corporate culture analytics:* Corporate culture data includes data that informs the norms, values and general behaviour of people in the organization.

    Analyzing corporate culture data may involve assessing current culture trends across the organization, as well as reviewing and defining the future state of the culture. The differences between the current state and the future state will help you develop the appropriate strategies to close the culture gaps.

    There are many types of culture measurement instruments that can be deployed for this analysis. The OCAI online tool[151] which was developed by Professors Kim Cameron and Robert Quinn, analyzes the six dimensions of culture in an organization. A stock-take of the current and desired culture is taken, and thereafter, a gap analysis is derived. This gap analysis helps organizations look at the areas of culture that can be strengthened to achieve alignment.

- *Leadership analytics:* Analyzing the effectiveness of an organization's leadership is vital for organizational success. In this type of analytics, we identify the traits of successful leaders needed for success and measure

---

[151] Kim Cameron and Robert Quinn, 'About the Organizational Culture Assessment Instrument (OCAI)', n.d.m., https://www.ocai-online.com/about-the-Organizational-Culture-Assessment-Instrument-OCAI. Accessed October 2021.

them through employee interviews, focus groups and surveys to extract relevant data.

Additionally, organizations such as SAP have started to treat the leadership trust index[152] as a measure of leadership effectiveness. According to SAP, building trust in leaders is essential for driving continuous high employee engagement. The leadership trust index is a measure that is derived from the Net Promoter Score (NPS) methodology.

The above examples illustrate the various types of people analytics that organizations can use to draw insights into their people resources.

Developing the Capabilities for People Analytics

In summary, what we would like to highlight is that you would need a set of different capabilities for developing an optimal people analytics function. While you may not have all the requisite skills needed to do so within your organization, the success of the function will be highly dependent on how you work in a multidisciplinary team comprising experts with the following capabilities:

1. *Business knowledge:* Business knowledge is fundamental for any HR analytics to be effective. In other words, HR analytics is all about the business and how HR can help it deliver performance. Which is why, it is fundamental

---

[152] SAP, *Integrated Reports 2019 on Work Performance*, available at: https://www.sap.com/integrated-reports/2019/en/social-performance.html. Accessed October 2021.

to understand the business challenges, key processes, in addition to an expertise in connecting HR to strategic company goals.

2. *Knowledge of Human Resources*: A scientific background in social sciences and an understanding of HR processes are necessary to combine traditional HR with people analytics expertise.

3. *Ability to perform data analysis:* You will also require statistical skills, as well as a basic knowledge of the different types of analytic methods. The ability to work with data using Excel, SPS or even a knowledge of Python or other programming languages will endow you with the ability to extract data for analysis.

4. *Basic understanding of IT:* While it is not necessary for you to be an IT expert, you need basic knowledge of data warehousing, business IT structures so that you can aggregate data from the different sources to draw your insights for decision-making.

5. *Data visualization and communication:* After obtaining the data, your ability to use visualization skills to organize the data into a succinct and concise form to tell a story, will help you persuasively draw attention to the insights that require managerial attention.

Figure 5.9 pulls together all the necessary capabilities for developing a people analytics function.

Managerial Implications for Building a People Analytics Function

The following points and recommendations can be key considerations to help you begin your people analytics journey:

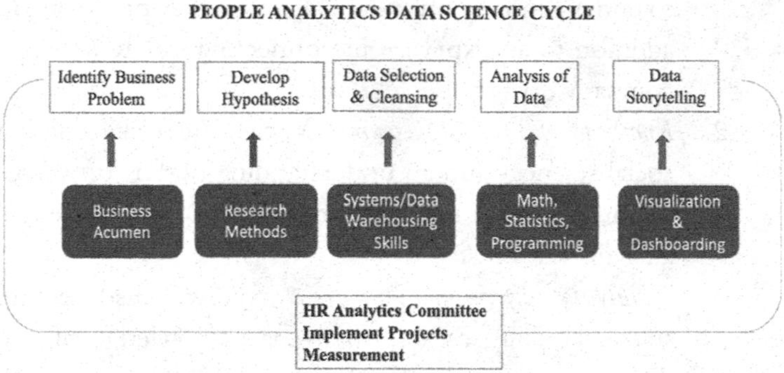

PEOPLE ANALYTICS DATA SCIENCE CYCLE

Figure 5.9: People Analytics Cycle

Source: Authors own

1. Assemble a capable people analytics team with the requisite skill sets. The team should be multi-disciplinary so they can work together to derive insights from data.
2. Set clear people goals and objectives that are aligned with the business strategy. Thereafter, develop the HR scorecard to define KPIs that can drive business performance.
3. Develop the employee journey map and establish clear data points for data collection and analysis.
4. Select one or two people analytics projects that have the greatest impact on the business. Define the goals of the projects so that the 'right' types of insights can be derived for decision-making.

Chapter 6

Hiring on Demand: A Security Organization Case Study

Applying systems thinking and supply chain management principles provides an alternative way to solve complex manpower issues.

Data can provide multiple ways to address talent management issues. In the previous chapters, we shared how to begin your analytics strategy by developing a clear strategy. We also expounded on the data science cycle and the steps needed to begin your people analytics journey. In this chapter, we will share a case study on how a security organization solved a complex workforce planning project through the clever use of data.

However, adopting a new and different lens is necessary to solve complex manpower resourcing issues. Large complex organizations with thousands of employees usually need a very systematic and methodological approach to managing manpower for optimization. This is no different from logistics companies utilizing efficient supply chains to manage the delivery of parcels across the globe.

The idea of using supply chain management principles is not new in the area of talent management. In his paper on 'Supply Chain Management Effective People Management', Indranil Mutsuddi[153] discussed the interdependencies between supply chain and HR management, and how by using an operations framework, the HR function can help organizations to effectively recruit and retain talent.

As shown in Figure 6.1, the HR function develops the employer brand, manages partnerships with external talent sourcing organizations and networks with professional bodies and educational institutes to hire the human capital for the organization. It is the interlink between the different HR functions and operations management which helps to ensure a constant balance between having too much or too little of the talent inventory.

It has also been shown that the use of an integrated stochastic resource planning of human capital supply chain can help with demand forecasting, risk-based capacity planning, supply evolution and optimization, and manage investments to balance human capital shortages.[154] Stochastic models use statistical analysis to review patterns in data. Several organizations,

---

[153] Indranil Mutsuddi, 'Supply Chain Management Effective People Management', *Journal of Operations Management*, 11 (4), November 2012, pp. 53–64.

[154] Heng Cao, Jianying Hu, Chen Jiang, Tarun Kumar, Ta-Hsin Li, Yang Liu, Yingdong Lu, Shilpa Mahatma, Aleksandra Mojsilović, Mayank Sharma, Mark S. Squillante, Yichong Yu, 'OnTheMark: Integrated Stochastic Resource Planning of Human Capital Supply Chains', *INFORMS Journal on Applied Analytics*, 41(5), 2011, pp.414–435, available at: https://doi.org/10.1287/inte.1110.0596. Accessed October 2021.

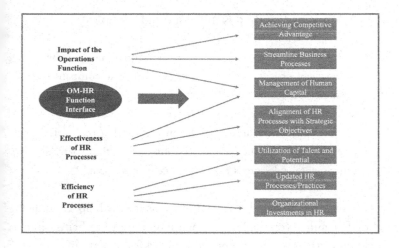

Figure 6.1: The OM–HR Function Interface Model

Source: Indranil Mutsuddi, 'Supply Chain Management Effective People Management'

including a German service provider,[155] started leveraging this idea to balance talent shortage against a cyclical demand. The firm started to employ dynamic modeling for workforce planning as previously, the company encountered issues of overcapacity during the lull periods and staff shortages during the peak periods, which caused a great deal of inconsistency and inefficient manpower deployment.

From these studies, we can see how the use of the supply chain concept for optimization and stochastic models can simulate talent flows in an analytics model for dynamic workforce planning.

---

[155] Andreas Größler and Alexander Zock, 'Supporting Long-Term Workforce Planning with a Dynamic Aging Chain Model—A Case Study from the Service Industry', *Human Resource Management*, 49 (5), September–October 2010, pp.829–848.

As explained by Brad Kamph, a supply chain expert:

> 'Another outside-the-box aspect of workforce management is business process optimization. Clearly, if a company's business processes are flawed, knowledge capture and knowledge transfer will be ineffective. Recruitment resources will be squandered, and attrition rates will stubbornly resist all efforts to lower them. Process optimization, then, plays a fundamental role across the workforce supply chain.'[156]

Dynamic modeling and stochastic models greatly help to predict shortfall and oversupplies in manpower supply chains, thus helping organizations optimize their workforce planning.

Singapore Example

Many years ago, I[157] worked for a large security organization that specializes in providing trained security personnel to both public and private sector organizations. On my first day of work as the Vice President of Human Resources, during a conversation with a human resources manager, I heard a response that I will never forget.

When the manager was queried as to his key role and targets as a recruitment manager, the response was 'the recruitment target is fifty security personnel but I have no clue how the number was derived'. As I probed about whether targets have

---

[156] Brad Kamph, 'Put the Dynamics of the Workforce Supply Chain to Work for You', *Power Magazine*, 15 January 2007, available at: https://www.powermag.com/put-the-dynamics-of-the-workforce-supply-chain-to-work-for-you/. Accessed October 2021.

[157] 'I' and 'my' in this context refer to Jaclyn Lee.

been met, the answer was a resounding 'no'. I further queried him on his resourcing methods, to which I heard, 'Well, I just put up an advertisement and I patiently wait in the recruitment center for candidates to show up'.

Needless to say, the business was always behind since there were manpower shortages. This was not only a culture issue— the organization had neither a process nor the tools to address this problem.

As I started speaking to the key stakeholders from sales, operations and deployment, pricing, and environmental health and safety, I came to the realization that this was a serious problem. The company had always faced constant labour shortages, high rates of sick leave, low efficiency ratios and had even lost many business opportunities due to manpower shortages.

As I began to analyze this problem, I explored the possibility of using a supply chain and operations model to solve this perennial problem. Taking inspiration from Stephen Miller,

'Workforce analytics can reduce workforce-related costs and risk. Through computer-based simulation modeling, you can explore alternative recruiting and staffing scenarios. This ensures you have the right kinds of talent and optimum number of individuals to achieve your goals with predictive accuracy.'[158]

---

[158] Stephen Miller. 'Applying Analytics can Enhance Workforce Planning', *Strategic HR Management*, 19 June 2016, available at: https://www.shrm.org/hr-today/news/hr-news/pages/workforce-analytics.aspx. Accessed September 2021.

At that time, the security manpower services industry played a very vital role in securing national borders and ensuring security and protection at key commercial and government buildings, national installations, critical water reserves, commercial complexes, banks, embassies, industrial facilities and so on. The security personnel work alongside with the police to provide safety and security to its citizens as their first line of defence. They also work together with the police to ensure public order at large national events. Another important role is the secure escorting of cash from banks to the hundreds of thousands of ATMs in Singapore. A significant amount of cash is handled on a daily basis by security personnel. Thus, a well-trained security workforce is crucial to ensure smooth and uninterrupted operations.

In general, large security companies in Singapore provide a suite of services, ranging from auxiliary police services, unarmed security services, cash escort and replenishment services, aviation security services, traffic control and other enforcement services. A key differentiator for any company in this business is to provide well-trained security manpower who can perform these specialized security services.

This industry has been plagued by a tight and shrinking labour force because of high turnover rates. Often, the demand outstrips supply. Because of this, it is not unexpected to say that the workforce is overstretched and overworked. The high burn-out rate does not help—adding on to the already-high attrition rate.

Additionally, there is a long cycle of time between the time a person is hired and the time the person is deployed on the ground. All new employees are required to go through stringent security screening, rigorous training, as well as testing. This further perpetuates the supply problem.

On-the-ground operations are often burdened by the following four issues:

- Scalability (there is sufficient manpower to feed business growth, address turnover issues, training incompletion and screening failures)
- Manpower availability
- Yield rates from training
- High turnover

As shown in the operational flow chart in Figure 6.2, the time taken from hire to deploy could be as long as twelve to sixteen weeks.

When the recruitment function is separated from operations, it leads to manpower shortages. Consequently, the industry can be stuck in a vicious cycle where demand constantly outstrips supply. To solve this problem, I began to employ a supply chain concept to address the fluctuations in demand and supply of manpower needed in the business. This process flow included the systematic procurement of manpower, deployment, right through the retention stage, in order to sustain the business.

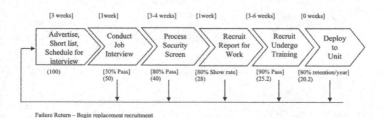

Figure 6.2: Recruitment Operational Flow

Source: Authors' own.

These principles were replicated to produce a just-in-time talent inventory that could scale up during times of need and size down during the lull periods.

To kickstart this operation, we set up a new unit called the 'Internal Sourcing Agency' (ISA). The ISA's role was to act as an in-house production plant specializing in the procurement of manpower. This unit worked directly with the sales and production units to forecast manpower demand with the lead time of at least six to nine months ahead of the business cycle (see Figure 6.3).

Starting with the sourcing function, the ISA would tap into its network to source manpower in the various specialized services, for example, Auxiliary Police Officers, Enforcement Officers, Security Officers, Aviation Screening Officers, and so on. The raw material—in this case, the untrained personnel—was put through a training framework to acquire the skills required for them to perform the job.

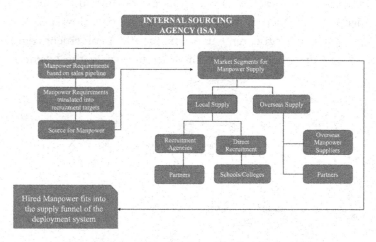

Figure 6.3: The Supply Chain of the ISA

Source: Authors' own

The trained manpower that has passed through the various security training and certifications is then deployed systematically through the company's delivery network of services. Any 'defective' manpower that could not pass the initial employment screening or proficiency tests, as well as those whom we could not obtain work permits for, were returned to the manpower suppliers. Returned manpower from customers included the personnel who did not meet the service standards required of the customer or were not confirmed due to lapses in their proficiency levels. Through this systematic framework, manpower supply became a real-time process that could meet demand of the business.

The ISA also used a manpower supply framework to source relevant manpower by collaborating with the business units to build a simple demand-and-supply matrix on a weekly basis, for ensuring that there were adequate security personnel to flow through the operations.

The demand-and-supply matrix examined factors such as holding strength, attrition, and new requirements for manpower. A net weekly recruitment figure was derived from this process for the ISA to source adequate supply of labor to meet customer needs.

The last part of the value chain is a robust HRM framework (see Figure 6.4) in which the HR functions support the HR Operations to deliver quality assurance and a high level of productivity. All these eventually lead to achieving business performance and meeting organizational milestones.

Data Collection Process

For such a project to work, we had to ensure that we collected the relevant data at each step. This also allowed us to measure and gauge the performance of each of the processes.

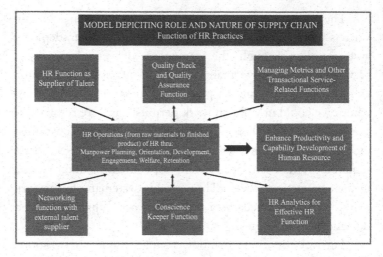

Figure 6.4: Human Capital Operations Framework

Source: Adapted Indranil Mutsuddi, 'Supply Chain Management'.[159]

The following list mentions the types of data that was collected:

ISA data

- Sources of recruitment to assess the effectiveness of each source
- Number of applications per month
- Actual candidates reached
- Actual candidates interviewed
- Actual candidates shortlisted
- Conversion rates of current hires
- Recruitment numbers per recruiter

---

[159] Mutsuddi, I. (2012). Supply Chain Management for Effective People Management: Issues and Challenges. IUP *Journal of Operations Management*, 11(4).

- Number of 'No shows'
- Number who passed training
- Percentage of demand met through supply

Sales pipeline data

- Number of projects tendered
- Conversion rate of tenders
- Actual sales clinched
- Number of employees needed in each category of the projects
- Timeline of new employees at each customer site that need to be deployed in the next six months

Deployment data

- Current duty posts
- Number of returnees from work site due to cessation of contracts
- Headcounts needed due to variation orders
- Turnover data
- Leave data

Projection data

- Actual number of contracts signed
- Actual passing rates of trainees ready for deployment
- Failure rates
- Handover data for deployment

The various data points culminate into the manpower planning demand-and-supply matrix. The final output from the ISA's numbers were then matched to the surplus shortfall of the demand–supply matrix to help recruiters proactively plan for their recruitment activities to meet the needs of the business.

Through a manpower planning supply chain model, the ISA was able to solve this resourcing issue within six months from the initial setup. The team ended up recruiting thousands of employees within a three-year timeframe and the company saw a multifold increase in revenue, while inking major contracts at the same time.

Other than developing these models, the team built a HR management framework to align the other key HR functions to support recruitment and retention of talents. The following data was collected to measure effectiveness and to derive insights:

- Employee satisfaction index
- Productivity data
- Profitability of business
- Revenue growth numbers
- Customer satisfaction rate
- Culture data
- Capability development data

Since the implementation of these data analytics initiatives, employee satisfaction consistently ranked at over 90 per cent for four consecutive years. Manpower shortages were drastically reduced while productivity rates went up. The company signed on a large government project amounting to millions of dollars and the ISA recruited close to 1,500 security personnel in nine months, to fulfill the contractual obligations.

This case study is an example of how principles of operations management and supply chain can be applied for solving complex manpower resourcing problems. The framework provided a continuous stream of manpower that could be fed into the business on a just-in-time basis and lead to a maximization of efficiencies. We would also like to highlight that this could not have been completed without a robust measurement system that incorporates data for effective recruitment, reward and retention of talents.

Managerial Implications

Incorporating systems thinking and modelling can help you to optimize your recruitment processes to maximize efficiency and scalability for your businesses. You can consider the following suggestions and ideas:

- Use the manpower supply chain concept and the principles in this chapter to review your current recruitment workflows.
- What are you currently measuring? Are you tracking all your key business metrics alongside your sales, operations, recruitment and training data to optimize your business?
- Finally, you can consider using the Indranil Mutsuddi's Human Capital Operations Framework to strengthen both the capacity and capability of the people resources within your organization. The framework provides a great end-to-end process for managing human capital operations.

Chapter 7

Transforming an Organization:
The OCBC Bank Case Study

A case study of how the OCBC Bank transformed into a predictive analytics engine.

The banking industry has been undergoing a lot of changes. From fintech to DeFi (decentralised finance), the changes in banking have been deep and wide. And traditional financial institutions and banks now operate side-by-side, with a new breed of online financial service providers.

Almost every aspect of banking from the way customers are managed right through to how investments are made and how employees are developed, have evolved significantly over the past few years. To stay ahead of the competition and survive this era of disruptive change, we believe that banks need to be adaptive and agile, and constantly innovating to offer new products and services.

However, inculcating a culture that supports innovation, adaptability and agility, and growth, is not merely enough for the survival of any bank. We believe that banks also need to embrace a strategy that is centred on people, culture and data, so that they can make better-informed decisions.

One of the first movers in embracing a data-centric strategy is the OCBC Bank. Even though OCBC's data journey commenced in 2013,[160] today, data is central to its continual transformation and preparation for the future of work.

How It Began

OCBC is one of Singapore's longest-established financial institutions. It was formed in 1932 after the merger of three local banks, of which, the oldest bank was established in 1912.[161] Today, OCBC has a global footprint and operates across nineteen countries. It is the second largest financial services institution in Southeast Asia by assets, and one of the world's highly rated banks, with an Aa1 rating by Moody's.[162]

OCBC first embarked on its data journey with customer analytics before it ventured into HR analytics. The bank's foray into HR data analytics started in 2013, when Cynthia Tan,

---

[160] Anushree Sharma, 'OCBC's Head of Group HR, Jason Ho on "Adaptable HR"', *People Matters*, 23 July 2020, https://www.peoplemattersglobal.com/article/hr-technology/ocbcs-head-of-group-hr-jason-ho-on-adaptable-hr-26426. Accessed June 2021.
[161] OCBC Bank, 'Group Business Overview', 2021, available at: https://www.ocbc.com/group/about-us/group-business. Accessed June 2021.
[162] Ibid.

then OCBC's Group Head of HR, introduced the concept of analytics to the bank.

At that time, HR analytics was still a novel and nascent concept—not only in Singapore, but across the world. Only 14 per cent of companies in the world could perform any sort of statistical analysis on employee data and only 4 per cent of companies could do any sort of predictive analytics.[163]

Cynthia Tan had her work cut out. While her team of HR professionals were proficient in the HR core skills, such as compensation and benefits, and recruitment and talent development, HR analytics was a new and foreign concept for most of them.[164] She knew that she needed help to transform her team from purely HR professionals to HR professionals who were proficient in data analytics. Given that the Group Customer Analytics Department (GCAD) had had a headstart in data analytics, she decided to reach out to this department for assistance. The GCAD department helped the HR team build an HR workflow model. This department also seconded an analytics headcount to help the HR team out.

Now a Trailblazer in HR Analytics

Fast forward to 2021. Not only is the bank known as a trailblazer in HR analytics, but OCBC has cemented its reputation as a leading global bank. The bank has launched many 'industry-first' initiatives and won multiple awards and accolades. The bank's

---

[163] Josh Bersin, 'Big Data in Human Resources: A World of Haves And Have-Nots', *Forbes*, 7 October 2013, available at: https://www.forbes.com/sites/joshbersin/2013/10/07/big-data-in-human-resources-a-world-of-haves-and-have-nots/?sh=cad265a200fd. Accessed June 2021.

[164] Interview with Jacinta Low, 23 March 2021 via Zoom.

efforts in HR analytics led to OCBC winning the prestigious 'Best HR Initiative at the Asian Banker Financial Technology Innovation Awards 2018'.[165]

One of OCBC's efforts is the 'HR in Your Pocket (HIP)' app—a new innovation and initiative that was launched in 2017. The app is a one-stop way for employees and managers to manage all things HR—things such as leave applications, understanding who's in the office and who's working from home, etc. The app, which was developed internally, is powered by an AI chatbot.[166]

The bank also launched Singapore's first industry-accredited data analytics course through the Institute of Banking and Finance. Members of the public can sign up for the course 'OCBC Bank's Data Certification Pathway',[167] as well as apply for training subsidies.

According to Jason Ho, the current Executive Vice President and Head of Group HR, a sound data strategy goes

---

[165] 'OCBC Bank Awarded The Best HR Initiative, Application or Programme for 2018 at The Asian Banker Financial Technology Innovation Awards 2018', *The Asian Banker*, 24 May 2018, available at: https://www.theasianbanker.com/updates-and-articles/ocbc-bank-awarded-the-best-hr-initiative-application-or-programme-for-2018-at-the-asian-banker-financial-technology-innovation-awards-2018. Accessed June 2021.

[166] 'OCBC's New HR App Includes AI-powered Chatbot', *Human Resources Online*, 7 June 2017, available at: https://www.humanresourcesonline.net/ocbcs-new-hr-app-includes-ai-powered-chatbot. Accessed June 2021.

[167] 'OCBC Bank's Data Certification Pathway is first data analytics and digital programme to obtain industry accreditation', Institute of Banking and Finance (IBF) Singapore, 24 August 2020, available at: https://www.ibf.org.sg/newsroom/Pages/NewsroomDetail.aspx?newsroomid=52&newsroomtypeid=b24530e6-feaa-4334-9708-2da5651f1b32. Accessed June 2021.

beyond having dashboards and reporting data.[168] It is also about making informed decisions that are backed by data. He articulated:

> 'With data analytics, we can enhance and validate on-the-ground information so that it's no longer purely qualitative. When information is backed by data, it becomes more objective and reason-driven, complementing the relationship-based information we have gathered to enable better decision-making.'[169]

OCBC has come a long way in its HR analytics journey. The HR analytics team is now comprised of four people, including a team lead, Jacinta Low, who is the Senior Vice President of HR and a champion of the bank's analytics journey. The team is further sub-divided into two sub-teams. While the two sub-teams have responsibilities related to data collection, cleansing and preparation for the different business units, one sub-team focuses on developing dashboards, whereas the other focuses on deriving insights and performing analysis.

Given OCBC's exemplary transformation journey, we thought it would be beneficial to share its data analytics journey with a wider audience. We are thankful to Jacinta Low for giving us the opportunity to interview her.

---

[168] Anushree Sharma, 'OCBC's Head of Group HR, Jason Ho on "Adaptable HR"', People Matters, 23 July 2020, https://www.peoplemattersglobal.com/article/hr-technology/ocbcs-head-of-group-hr-jason-ho-on-adaptable-hr-26426. Accessed June 2021.

[169] Nelissa Hernandez, 'Jason Ho: A Digital Strategy is Also About People', Infocomm Media Development Authority, 22 May 2019, available at: https://www.imda.gov.sg/news-and-events/impact-news/2018/02/jason-ho-a-digital-strategy-is-also-about-people. Accessed June 2021.

Jacinta Low
Senior Vice President of HR, OCBC Bank

Setting the Foundation for HR Analytics Transformation

There were several questions that were on the top of our minds when we met with Jacinta Low:

- How did OCBC transform itself so quickly in HR analytics?
- What were the key drivers of success?
- What were some examples of the HR analytics projects?

Low told us that starting from ground zero was no easy feat. It involved lots of education and training to reskill the HR team.

Furthermore, she informed us that when Cynthia Tan first embarked on the analytics journey, she was very clear about the HR data transformation plan. Establishing credibility was at the forefront of her strategy because it was a critical component that was necessary to garner buy-in from her peers on the executive team. Which was why she focused on getting quick wins at the start of the journey.

Cynthia Tan was also laser-focused on the objective of data analytics—to 'help the business solve their human resource challenges by understanding data'.[170]

> 'We wanted to focus on quick wins so that we could establish the credibility, interest and demand for HR data analytics. We had a workshop to ascertain what mattered to the business. This workshop was attended by business heads, HR business partners and the COEs (Centres of Excellence).'

She mobilized her team to adopt a test-and-learn and an experimental approach, so that she and her team could course-correct along the way. The test-and-learn approach, or what Jason Ho, the current Group Head of HR, calls, the 'learn fast, fail fast, succeed fast'[171] approach, is still in place today for the HR analytics team at OCBC to continually learn and grow.

HR Information Systems

Any discussion about data analytics would not be complete without a discussion on the underlying HRIS. Given that OCBC's HR team wanted to show results quickly, the team

---

[170] Interview with Jacinta Low, March 23, 2021, via Zoom.
[171] Anushree Sharma, 'OCBC's Head of Group HR, Jason Ho on "Adaptable HR"', People Matters, 23 July 2020, https://www.peoplemattersglobal.com/article/hr-technology/ocbcs-head-of-group-hr-jason-ho-on-adaptable-hr-26426. Accessed June 2021.

decided to work with whatever data they had at hand, to solve the business challenges and problems.

'We worked with whatever data we had at hand. We scrubbed it thoroughly before developing a POC (Proof of Concept) to push it out to the business leaders to get their feedback. The test-and-learn approach has been our initial approach and is still the approach we adopt to build the pipeline of data for deriving insights.'[172]

The approach of leveraging existing data was against the grain of what top analytics organizations would do at the time—which would typically entail building a centralized analytics COE—a process that could take up to eighteen months to build. But the HR team did not have the time, the resources or the budget to do so. Hence, the plan proceeded with working with the available data in OCBC's HRIS.

Even though eight years have passed since its first analytics project, the bank still adopts a decentralised best-of-breed approach for its HRIS.[173] Its core HR system remains in Oracle. The Taleo system is used for recruitment. Cornerstone is used for training and Kincentric, for employee engagement.

While this approach has allowed the bank to select the best and most optimal IT application for the different HR functions, the challenge of the decentralized approach lies in data extraction and preparation. Which is why the bank has decided to conduct a review and audit on its HRIS. The review of the HRIS has also come at a time when the bank is considering venturing into big data to further strengthen its predictive analytics capabilities. Low explained:

---

[172] Interview with Jacinta Low, March 23, 2021, via Zoom.
[173] Ibid.

'We are working to bring in big data, including email data, into our data strategy. We conducted a POC back in 2017 with Trustsphere, a network analysis consultancy, to understand email behavioural data, including when employees are logging in and logging off.

We also wanted insights into these important questions:

- Is burn-out an issue for the bank?
- Are there any key influencers in the bank? And who are they?
- How strong is the network of the bank's high potential employees?' [174]

Risk Prediction Model for Employee Attrition

The very first model that was developed was the 'Risk Prediction Model of Employee Attrition'. This model can predict employee attrition to about a 75 per cent degree of accuracy. [175]

Whilst the model was developed eight years ago, it is still in use by the bank today. And it has helped HR and the business leaders to avoid and reduce regrettable attrition or retain 'people the bank doesn't want to lose'. [176]

Essentially, the model helps the bank answer two important questions about attrition:

1.   How can OCBC predict employee attrition?

---

[174] Ibid.

[175] Ibid.

[176] The HR Space, 'Using Data Analytics and Tech in HR', 2018, available at: https://www.thehrspace.com.au/news/using-data-analytics-and-tech-in-hr/27721/. Accessed June 2021.

2. And conversely, what are the factors that would make people stay?

With this model, the HR team can categorize employees into three groups of high-, medium-, and low-risk levels of attrition, and use the information to focus their efforts especially on retaining the employees in the high-risk category. Efforts such as ring-fencing this group of employees via constant dialogue between the manager and the identified employee, have been initiated. In implementing these initiatives, OCBC has been able to stem the attrition of the high-risk group of employees, consequently reducing attrition to a level that is below the industry average.

In building the model, the HR analytics team did not rely only on one source system for the data. Jacinta Low elaborated the steps in detail:

'We went to our HR core system to aggregate data to build the model. We looked at training data, sick leave, supervisor tenure, employee tenure, gender, rank, performance data of the individual, manager and colleagues, as well as studied the impact of pay increases.

We also analyzed how the different sets of data interacted with one another. After conducting some in-depth analysis, we came to a conclusion that there were two factors— training and upward mobility of the immediate supervisor and colleagues—that had a lot of bearing on employee attrition.'[177]

Trend-Spotting the Under-Performing Organizations

Other than building models, the HR analytics team also helps to value-add to the business by performing trend analyses.

---

[177] Ibid.

One such trend analysis that was conducted was to understand the factors driving sales performance. Two insights emerged from this trend analysis. It was found that high performing sales organizations were led by managers who constantly 'rah rah' or 'pump up' their organizations. The other insight revealed that the managers of the high-performing sales organizations frequently provided coaching to their teams.[178]

In order to raise the overall performance of the sales organization, these insights were shared with the lower-performing sales organizations. Consequently, these leaders were able to boost their teams' sales performance while at the same time, reduce attrition.

Resourcing Model

The next key model that was developed is the Resourcing Model. Before the involvement of the analytics team, the tracking, monitoring and measurement of the recruiting process was done manually using Microsoft Excel.

The Resourcing Model was initially built to understand the time-to-hire process, specifically to measure the number of days taken to close an open position. Another objective of the model was to measure the performance of the individual recruiters and gain insights on the 'chokes' or barriers that were causing recruitment delays.

Today, the model not only measures effectiveness metrics, such as the metrics outlined above, but it also measures efficiency metrics, such as the quality of hire (Figure 7.1).

---

[178] Ibid.

Previous Quality of Hire Metric

Quality of hire = (1 - Employees left this month before six-month tenure)/Employees hired this month

New Quality of Hire Metric

Quality of hire = Employees hired six months ago who are still at OCBC/Employees hired this month

To provide visibility to the recruitment process, the HR analytics team went one step further to develop a dynamic dashboard using QlikView. This Resourcing dashboard, which is traffic-light coded, highlights the issues requiring attention using data visualization (Figure 7.2).

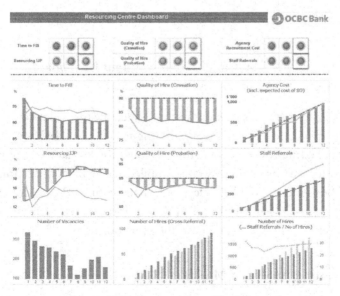

Figure 7.2: Resourcing Dashboard

Source: OCBC Bank (Figures shown are for illustrative purposes only).

Figure 7.3: Candidate Movement Dashboard

Source: OCBC Bank (Figures shown are for illustrative purposes only).

A further enhancement to the model saw the inclusion of a Candidate Movement Dashboard (Figure 7.3). The dashboard is a marked improvement over the previous process that was manual and tedious, as updates were compiled either by consolidating responses over email or telephone. This dashboard can provide a quick overview of the job openings and the corresponding recruiters who are working on the open positions.

Training Analytics Model

OCBC's training strategy 'We see you' communicates to its employees that the bank will provide everything from 'learning content, priorities, processes, policies, infrastructure and systems'[179] to enable its employees to continually learn, unlearn and relearn. There are over 1,400 courses and training programmes that are offered to employees.[180] The programmes have been carefully curated to future-proof the employees, 'We want our employees to be proactive in looking at themselves and asking—will I still be relevant five, ten, twenty years down the road, and what can I do to stay ahead?'[181]

The bank invests a significant amount of its budget on reskilling. Recently, 15 per cent of its employees who are above fifty years of age, were reskilled in digital skills.[182] The bank selected 1,300 of its employees to participate in the 'Professional Conversion Programme' so that they can take on new and enhanced roles by 2022.[183]

The bank has also pledged to invest S$20 million[184] and place 29,000 of its employees in the 'OCBC Future Smart Programme',

---

[179] OCBC Bank, 'Investing in People: How OCBC Bank Unlocks its Employees' Potential', eFinancialCareers, 10 January 2019, available at: https://www.efinancialcareers.sg/news/2019/01/investing-people-ocbc-bank-unlocks-employees-potential-sc.Accessed June 2021.

[180] Aditi Sharma Kalra, 'Q&A: Jason Ho, Executive VP and Head of Group HR, OCBC Bank', *Human Resources Online*, 30 May 2018, available at: https://www.humanresourcesonline.net/qa-jason-ho-executive-vp-and-head-of-group-hr-ocbc-bank. Accessed June 2021.

[181] Ibid.

[182] Ibid.

[183] Tripartite Alliance, *Human Capital Partnership Quarterly e-Bulletin*, Number 16, April 2021, https://www.tal.sg/tafep/-/media/TAL/Tafep/Resources/Publications/Files/2021/HCP-E-bulletin-Issue-16_April-June-2021.pdf. Accessed June 2021.

[184] OCBC Bank, 'Investing in People: How OCBC Bank Unlocks its Employees' Potential', eFinancialCareers, 10 January 2019, available at: https://www.efinancialcareers.sg/news/2019/01/investing-people-ocbcbank-unlocks-employees-potential-sc.Accessed June 2021. At an exchange rate of $US1 = S$1.34; S$20 million = US$14.9 million.

a flagship programme that aims to increase capabilities in seven digital domains,[185] including (i) digital business models and ecosystems, (ii) technology and data, (iii) customer centricity, (iv) new risks, (v) marketing and communications, (vi) the way we work, and (vii) leadership in the future world. This programme is now in its second phase, and includes a comprehensive suite of training modules on sustainability.[186]

Another important course that was launched is the OCBC's Data Certification Pathway Course. This course was designed to raise the overall proficiency and data literacy of its 29,000-strong workforce, specifically, in programming and coding, data governance, data storytelling and visualization, data computation and modelling, and data mining.[187] And as of August 2020, some 200 OCBC employees have taken the course.[188]

Considering the importance of training and development, the analytics team was tasked at the beginning of 2021 to develop a Training Analytics Model to ascertain the impact of training on promotion, performance and attrition, as well as to learn more about the characteristics of 'active learners'. Active learners are widely believed to be better performers with higher

---

[185] OCBC Bank, 'OCBC Bank Launches Digital Transformation Programme For 29,000 Employees', *Fintech Singapore*, 8 May 2018, available at: https://fintechnews.sg/19664/fintech/ocbc-bank-digital-transformation-programme-for-29000-employees/. Accessed June 2021.

[186] OCBC Bank, 'OCBC Bank Rolls Out Comprehensive Sustainability Training as it Adds More Than 50 New Jobs in ESG Push', 8 July 2021, available at: https://www.ocbc.com/group/media/release/2021/sustainability_training.page? Accessed June 2021.

[187] OCBC Bank, 'OCBC Bank Launches Digital Transformation Programme For 29,000 Employees', Fintech Singapore, 8 May 2018, available at: https://fintechnews.sg/19664/fintech/ocbc-bank-digital-transformationprogramme-for-29000-employees/. Accessed June 2021.

[188] Ibid.

productivity. Specifically, the training model aims to answer the following questions:

- What is the profile of an active learner?
- How can the bank have more active learners?
- Can the bank replicate the number of active learners?

OCBC's HIP (HR in Your Pocket) App

As mentioned earlier, another innovation by the HR Analytics team was the development of the OCBC's HR in Your Pocket (HIP) app. With support from the IT team, the HR team was proud to be the first team in Singapore to launch the first AI-enabled HR mobile app in 2017.[189]

The app leverages an AI chatbot 'Buddy' at the frontend and is integrated with the core HRIS at the backend. It took the team a mere eight weeks to develop a functioning app to give the bank's employees easy and instantaneous access to HR-related services and information, including leave applications, tracking of employee medical and lifestyle expense reimbursement claims, internal job postings, and the bank's internal directory. Managers can also easily approve leave and get visibility on who's on deck and who's on vacation.

Unlike a typical app that provides broad-based robotic answers, this app is customized and tailored to the individual employee's unique profile. The app also leverages natural processing language. It functions like Apple's Siri, Amazon's Alexa or Microsoft's Cortana and 'talks' to employees like a human being.[190] It has been shown to address at least 90 per cent of all

---

[189] Interview with Jacinta Low, March 23, 2021, via Zoom.
[190] The Asian Banker, ` OCBC Bank awarded The Best HR Initiative, Application or Programme for 2018 at *The Asian Banker* Financial

employees' HR-related queries, thus saving OCBC a whopping 50 per cent in manpower costs if headcount were hired for this very function.[191]

The app also provides a functionality for employees to inform their managers if they are well. Employees can also indicate whether they are working from home or working onsite.

Given the high adoption of the app, the HR analytics team plans to add enhancements to its future versions. Enhancements such as providing training and development on the app so that employees can learn on-the-go.[192] The team also envisages including more manual and laborious HR administrative work to be addressed by the app.

Eye on the Future

While OCBC has accomplished much and transformed its HR function with data analytics, the bank recognizes that continuous transformation is what it needs to stay ahead of the curve. Just as how Jacinta Low looks to the following questions to guide the forward path for the analytics team, so too can we:

1.   What are the capabilities required?
2.   What are the business requirements?
3.   What is required to add value to the business?[193]

Technology Innovation Awards 2018', *The Asian Banker*, 2018, https://www.theasianbanker.com/updates-and-articles/ocbc-bank-awarded-the-best-hr-initiative-application-or-programme-for-2018-at-the-asian-banker-financial-technology-innovation-awards-2018. Accessed August 2021.
[191]   Ibid.
[192]   Interview with Jacinta Low, March 23, 2021, via Zoom.
[193]   Excerpt from 'OCBC's Head of Group HR, Jason Ho on "Adaptable HR"', LaptrinhX, 20 July 2020, available at: https://laptrinhx.com/ocbc-s-head-of-group-hr-jason-ho-on-adaptable-hr-2563107920/. Accessed June 2021.

Chapter 8

Building a New World Organization: SUTD Case Study

SINGAPORE UNIVERSITY OF
TECHNOLOGY AND DESIGN

Developing competencies for the new world of work will require a focus on multi-disciplinary learning coupled with innovative, personal and creative skills.

Technology is disrupting everything and is changing everything—from the way we consume to the way we work, play and learn. The world in which we work is moving at an accelerated pace and more so after the onset of the coronavirus pandemic. Continuous transformation as in the case of OCBC bank will be imperative for the organizations of the future.

Since the start of the pandemic, digital adoption has skyrocketed. The explosion of digital transformation has resulted in the emergence of a plethora of new skills that are critical for the future of work. Kate Whiting,[194] a senior writer at the World Economic Forum found that 50 per cent of all employees will need reskilling by 2025 as adoption of technology increases and critical thinking and problem solving become the top skills required by employers.

As such, the model of higher education has to change. In her book, *Singapore's Higher Education Systems in the Era of the Fourth Industrial Revolution*, Nancy Gleason showed that information transfer is no longer a viable form of education for employment and having a career. And today's institutes of higher learning (IHLs) will need to collaborate more with industry and government agencies.

There are three reskilling strategies that are specific to IHLs in the latest report by the Committee of the Future Economy,[195] established by the Singapore's Ministry of Trade and Industry. The three strategies that are critical for success are:

- Deepening and diversifying international connections
- Acquiring and utilizing deep skills
- Building strong digital capabilities

In anticipation of the future of work, Singapore's fourth autonomous university, Singapore University of Technology and Design (SUTD), was set up in 2009 with the mission of

---

[194] Kate Whiting, 'These are the top 10 job skills of tomorrow—and how long it takes to learn them', World Economic Forum, 21 October 2020, available at: https://www.weforum.org/agenda/2020/10/top-10-work-skills-of-tomorrow-how-long-it-takes-to-learn-them/. Accessed September 2021.

[195] Ministry of Trade and Industry, *Report of the Committee on the Future Economy*, February 2017, available at: https://www.mti.gov.sg/-/media/MTI/Resources/Publications/Report-of-the-Committee-on-the-Future-Economy/CFE_Full-Report.pdf. Accessed October 2021.

advancing knowledge and nurturing technically grounded leaders who can solve complex vital societal needs through technology and design.

The university's core mission is to develop and inspire a generation of entrepreneurs who have the potential to make breakthroughs in Singapore's architecture, engineering, technology, design and software industries. Unlike other traditional universities, SUTD's unique curriculum embraces a blend of teaching methods, approaches and perspectives in small-sized classrooms, and inculcates an 'And World' and design-thinking mentality to enable students to hold 'two opposed ideas in the mind at the same time, and still retain the ability to function'.[196]

The academic programmes adopt an outside-in approach, and look to industry needs and the challenges of the world as its starting point. Another unique aspect of SUTD is its focus on technology innovation and 'Big-D' (Big-Design and Humanities). The university focuses on open-ended problem solving and active learning by providing hands-on experience, including getting students to build prototypes to test their ideas and concepts.

From the outset, SUTD was designed to have a fluid structure with no boundaries. Until today, SUTD's approach fosters multidisciplinary and inter-disciplinary collaboration, while still focusing on the foundational disciplines that are mathematics, basic sciences, architecture, computer science, and mechanical, electrical and other fields of engineering.

Its curriculum is centred on products, services and systems, and structured on the four core pillars or areas of specialization,

---

[196] Roger L. Martin, *The Opposable Mind: Winning Through Integrative Thinking* (Boston: Harvard Business Press, 2009).

comprising Engineering Product Development, Engineering Systems Design, Information Systems and Design, and Architecture and Sustainable Design. A fifth programme was introduced in 2020, which is 'Design and Artificial Intelligence'. The programmes are complemented by the clusters of Humanities and Social Sciences, as well as Science, Mathematics and Technology.

The concept of no boundaries and fluidity can also be seen in the design of the new SUTD campus that was completed in December 2014. A large proportion of the campus real estate was designed to encourage collaboration and teamwork. Instead of clearly defined 'pillar' floors or spaces, team members who work on the same project are seated together, even though they may be specializing in different pillars. For example, the team working on 'sustainable cities' is seated together on the same floor, despite each of them having different pillars of specialization. This fluid structure and way of collaboration has enabled the team to not only fully immerse themselves in design thinking, but also adopt multiple perspectives in problem solving.

Table 8.1 below outlines the vision and design of SUTD that is in contrast to the other traditional universities. It also shows SUTD's alignment to the future of work.

To achieve the university's mission, vision and strategic goals, it was decided that top-tier global and local talents who possessed the required competencies and expertise need to be sourced and attracted to work at SUTD. SUTD began its talent search by adopting a local and international strategy as early as 2010.

The university also focused on growing its research capabilities and bench strength. The intensive recruitment effort has paid off and the university now has a total of 170 faculty members from

Table 8.1: The Vision and Design of SUTD versus Other Traditional Universities

	Traditional University	SUTD
Organizational Structure	Hierarchical and territorial	Flat and agile with no schools, but instead, pillars of specialization, which form the main core of the university
Operating Model	Decentralization	Shared services
Student Interaction	Big lecture series to achieve economies of scale	Small cohort-size classrooms to achieve intimacy of interaction
Student Learning	Theoretical	A strong theoretical foundation coupled with a hands-on interactive experience that is interlaced with internships and practice

Research	Narrowly Focused	Multi-disciplinary, focused on innovation and creativity (development and improvement of artifacts) rather than only description or explanation
Faculty Recruitment	Decentralized with a narrow focus	Decentralization at the first level of screening, but centralization when it comes to the decision to hire. The president chairs the final selection committee together with a multi-disciplinary team to ensure that each faculty hired has the potential to collaborate across the different specializations
Faculty Governance	Dominant in faculty self-governance	Mixed faculty governance with specifically chartered work teams on key projects that may also include administrative staff

thirty different countries, as well as 400 researchers working on different innovative research projects. The university also has a strong team of administrators to support the faculty and the researchers.

Workforce Development Strategy for Phase 1

Although the vision and mission of SUTD have always aligned with the new world of work, many of its initial key stakeholders have come from a traditional university environment. As highlighted by Clayton Christenson and Henry Eyring in their book, *The Innovative University*,[197] in the spirit of honouring tradition, universities hang on to past practices to the point of 'imperilling' their futures. They do not reinvent their curriculum to better prepare students for the increasing demands of the world of work.

Recognizing that stakeholders could easily revert back to traditional university culture, the university embarked upon a culture exercise very early on in its history. The development and integration of a strong organizational culture that is consistent with SUTD's vision was foundational during this phase of SUTD's workforce development strategy.

The first culture project included many dialogue sessions between the senior management team and the board. It was from these dialogues that the five core values of the institution, 'leadership', 'integrity', 'passion', 'collaboration' and 'creativity', were identified. The senior leaders and board members carefully chose these values to drive the behaviours of the university's existing and future employees. The core values also set the tone for what SUTD cares about, and conveys the expectations of its employees.

---

[197] Christensen, Clayton M. and Henry J. Eyring, *The Innovative University: Changing the DNA of Higher Education from the Inside Out* (New Jersey: John Wiley & Sons, 2011).

Next in the culture transformation process was the culture alignment process to support SUTD's vision and mission. In February 2013, thirteen key members of the management team and several senior academic and administrative staff worked together to determine the existing culture and defined what the leaders collectively saw as the culture SUTD should aspire to. The team leveraged the Organizational Culture Assessment Instrument (OCAI), a tool that is based on the Competing Values Framework.[198]

The Competing Values Framework is a robust, tried-and-tested method that was designed to help organizations diagnose and make proper changes to their culture. This framework is based on two dimensions. The first dimension hones in on organizational focus, ranging from an internal focus on people to an external focus, or market focus. The second dimension represents the contrast between a structure for stability and control, and a structure for flexibility and change. Together, the two dimensions form the four quadrants that represent the following four culture archetypes:

1. **Hierarchy:** a culture that promotes formal processes and procedures
2. **Market:** a culture that is focused on the external environment and is results-oriented and competitive
3. **Adhocracy:** a culture that is nimble, flexible, dynamic and entrepreneurial
4. **Clan:** a family culture orientation that is internally focused but flexible

---

[198] Kim S. Cameron and Robert E. Quinn, *Diagnosing and Changing Organizational Culture: Based on The Competing Values Framework*, Third edition (San Francisco: Jossey-Bass, 2011).

When the culture alignment process was extended to a wider audience, including the university population, the whole university voted for an Adhocracy and Clan culture.

This led to a series of workshops and projects where the desired culture was cultivated. This culture effort, which was supported by the university's learning and development strategy, was reinforced for over nine years through multiple programmes and strategic activities (see Figure 8.1). The programmes included four sub-components of leadership development, culture development, core training plus self-directed learning.

Phase 1 resulted in many achievements and successes for SUTD. The strong unifying culture that was established at the beginning has held importance for all of SUTD's stakeholders including students, faculty and staff, who have diverse backgrounds and come from different disciplinary, national, cultural and institutional origins.

Given the changing expectations of the world of work, you can say that the SUTD's culture journey is a journey that many universities must embark upon so that they can align themselves to future trends.

Workforce Development Strategy for Phase 2

Phase 2 of the workforce development strategy was centred on research. In this phase, the president, together with the board and the senior leadership team, began identifying the core research areas for preparing SUTD for the new world of work. The industry areas of aviation, healthcare and cities, supported by horizontal technology of artificial intelligence and design were identified.

Following this process, the new workforce development strategy included acquiring local and international talents in the growth areas. Other talent programmes such as the Faculty

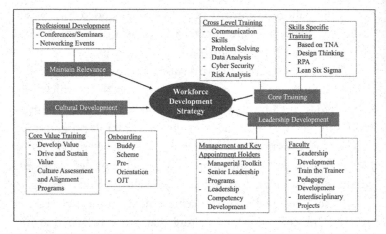

Figure 8.1: Workforce Development Strategy: Phase 1
Source: Authors' own.

Early-Career Award Scheme, were introduced. The purpose of the scheme is to identify newly graduated, high-potential Ph.D. candidates with promising research acumen to join SUTD as faculty fellows, as well as to build the talent pipeline for faculty members. A faculty fellow is offered the opportunity to become an Assistant Professor if he or she performs well in the three-year fellowship programme.

The university also took the opportunity to develop the leadership competency framework. With support from a professional consulting firm, the HR team and the senior management spent six months working with internal stakeholders to identify critical success factors and behaviours for SUTD leaders. Six competencies emerged from this exercise and they were as follows:

- **Thinking strategically:** Focus on broader, longer-term purposes and issues, and create strategies and plans for the university. At higher levels, has the ability to develop a strategy that conceptualizes and incorporates purpose as well as complex issues in the environment, and provides a clear concept for the future, which people understand and are enabled to move forward by.

- **Driving impact:** Drives towards superior outcomes for the university with speed and action. Pushes to meet or exceed requirements of deliverables with a sense of urgency. At higher levels, transforms what the university can do, enabling it to punch above its weight.

- **Collaborating and influencing:** Engages with others over whom they have no authority. Creates partnerships and compromises appropriately for results, rather than giving in. At the higher levels, creates enduring partnerships across barriers.

- **Innovating:** Tries out new things amidst ambiguities, even at the risk of failure, as long as one can learn from them or eliminate bad options in the future. At the higher levels, it is about taking deliberate, calculated risks with large potential payoffs. Thus clearly differentiating SUTD from other institutions.

- **Leading people:** Manages, focuses, and empowers team members. Communicates, delegates and monitors deliverables. Develops people in the long term. At higher levels, creates empowered leaders to execute efficiently through the layers of the university.

- **Managing stakeholders:** Responding to, supporting and anticipating stakeholder needs. At higher levels, changes the approach to stakeholders, including organizational mindset, processes and systems.

Figure 8.2 illustrates how the different components come together in Phase 2 of the workforce development strategy as described above.

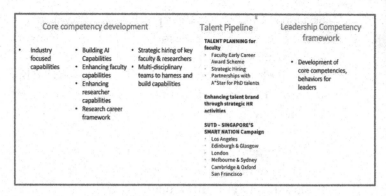

Figure 8.2:   Workforce Development Strategy: Phase 2

Source: Authors' own.

Workforce Development Strategy for Phase 3

The first and second phases of SUTD's workforce development strategy helped the university claim its position as the fifth most influential institution in the world for telecommunications,[199] achieve a high employment rate of over 95 per cent for its students and produce a strong research and publications track record. SUTD was also recognized as the top university on the list of 'Emerging Engineering Universities in the World' in a benchmark study that was conducted by the Massachusetts Institute for Technology (MIT).[200]

---

[199]   Toh Wen Li, 'NTU, SUTD and A*Star Among Top in World for Research in Various Fields: Study', *The Straits Times*, 3 October 2017, available at: https://www.straitstimes.com/singapore/education/ntu-sutd-and-astar-among-top-in-world-for-research-in-various-fields-study. Accessed October 2021.

[200]   Dr Ruth Graham, *The Global State of the Art in Engineering Education*, MIT, March 2018, available at: https://jwel.mit.edu/sites/mit-jwel/files/assets/files/neet_global_state_of_eng_edu_180330.pdf. Accessed October 2021.

In line with the growth trend of the university in the last ten years, the amount of administrative workload and processes also began to increase, resulting in inefficiencies. It also prevented administrators from focusing on the more value-added activities. This was why a strategic workforce planning and analysis project was initiated at the beginning of 2018 to optimize and effectively deploy administrative resources to meet the growing needs of the university. The project also aimed to establish a clear understanding of the current workforce capacity and capabilities, as well as future workforce requirements based on SUTD's 2023 growth plan.

The taskforce undertook the following key steps:

1. Gathered information about the roles and responsibilities of every function, using which they identified the gaps and the unnecessary work, as well as listed the areas with potential for improvement.
2. Identified the opportunities for redesigning the way work was carried out to determine what could either be digitized or eliminated altogether.
3. Collated an inventory of current competencies.
4. Identified future-ready competencies for improving staff development and retention, and work–life balance.

The six-month-long project involved every department in the university. And a detailed analysis was conducted on the job scope and duties of each administrative position. Raw data was collected from ninety-seven sub-organizational units that showed that there existed 1,328 main activities, 4,323 sub-activities and 18,000 activity steps, amounting to 1,154,331 activity hours.

In analyzing the activity data, the workforce planning taskforce uncovered the following:

- **Too much time was spent on procurement activities:** 11 per cent of the administrative staff's time was spent on procurement activities that were onerous and had many process steps.
- **Too much time was spent on reviews:** Administrators spent more than 35 per cent of their time on reviews, verifications and approvals that were long and tedious
- **Potential for automation:** 16 per cent of all the administrative activities that support the operation of the university could be automated. These activities spanned across finance, procurement and facilities management, to name a few.

The final step of the project involved capability development, specifically to identify the future skills for SUTD's Phase 3 Strategic Plan. The analysis showed the competency gaps that needed to be addressed:

- Problem-solving skills
- Analytical skills
- Communication skills
- Change management skills
- Facilitation skills

And as for the skills that needed development for running an effectively administered organization, the gaps were found in:

- Data analytics and visualization skills

- Project management skills
- Agile thinking skills

Resulting Action Plans

Other than providing insights for driving effective workforce planning and capability development for the university's third phase of growth, the project showed that resource sharing and synergies needed to be improved across the university. There was also a need to promote greater efficiency by reinventing and improving processes, as well as automating non-value-added processes.

This led the senior leadership team to set broad directions and a roadmap, for which, recommendations included a review of the university's IT strategy and roadmap for digital transformation. A detailed user analysis followed. And efforts were made to integrate systems on common platforms.

Fast forward to today. Many of the rejuvenation projects have commenced and as we write this chapter in October 2021, SUTD is embarking on a digital transformation effort in both the finance and human resources departments to migrate the existing systems to cloud-based platforms to provide better functionalities to users.

The university has also revamped the procurement processes and developed a bespoke procurement system that has reduced the multiple tedious steps in the procurement process. And training has been conducted to educate people on the new and improved process.

Furthermore, lean six-sigma project teams were formed to review the process steps and improve efficiencies in the administrative processes. A business excellence expert was hired and robotic process automation (RPA) was deployed to automate repetitive financial processes. A community practice was also set up to promote best practices in driving efficiency improvements.

Additionally, the human capital development team initiated a university-wide data science course to equip all employees with basic data science capabilities, as well as design thinking skills.

As of today, the third phase of transformation is yet to be completed as it is still a continuous process of training and framing the right projects for analysis.

Managerial Implications

In the post pandemic world, disruptions will become more frequent. Adaptability and flexibility will be key for organizations to survive in the future.

Hence, workforce planning is critical for ensuring that organizations have the right skills and talents to drive organizational strategy.

Here are some additional suggestions and ideas for effective workforce planning:

- Start by developing your diagnostic analytics capability. You can then combine different data sources to look at your current capabilities.
- Conduct scenario planning by creating different scenarios to understand the future skills that will be needed.
- Conduct a gap analysis to identify the gap between current and future skills.
- Develop a roadmap to upskill the whole workforce.
- When conducting workforce planning, it is important to bear in mind the '4 Rs':
    ◦ **Right size:** No vacancies and organization should not be overstaffed.

- ○ **Right shape:** Critical competencies are in place and there is succession planning.
- ○ **Right agility:** Foster an agile, resilient and flexible workforce.
- ○ **Right cost:** Ensure cost efficiency through detailed mapping of each job scope to avoid duplication of resources.
- Lastly, ensure you engage the key stakeholders in the process and get change champions to help you on your journey of workforce transformation.

Chapter 9

Integrating People, Data and Culture: SAP Case Study

A case study describing the innovative HR practices that SAP uses to integrate its people, data and culture strategy.

The integration of people, data and culture sets the foundation for success as described in the preceding chapters. This chapter shares the case study of SAP, an organization that has successfully integrated all three elements.

SAP, a global software company headquartered in Walldorf, South of Germany, has a vision of helping customers optimize their business processes and run an intelligent enterprise. SAP was started in 1972 by five former IBM employees who had a dream of creating a standard application software for real-time business processing.

The company started with a single customer and a handful of employees. Forty-nine years later, it has a customer base of 440,000 customers in more than 180 countries and an employee count of 102,430. Its global revenue in 2020 was €27.34 billion (US$31.74 billion).[201] Today, 77 per cent of all business transactions in the world touch an SAP system.

SAP has also been lauded as one of the best places to work—the company has received 125 'employer of choice' awards across the world. The list of awards includes thirty awards for best workplace, twenty-two awards for equality, ten awards for work–life balance, and nine recognitions related to early talent recruitment and development.

Which is why we wanted to understand: What is the remarkable force behind SAP's success?

In our interview with Renata Janini Dohmen, the Global Head for Early Career Talent Attraction at SAP, she shared that it has to do with the way SAP manages people, processes and technology, that has resulted in a highly engaged workforce and ultimately, performance.

SAP is an organization that places a high level of emphasis on being people-first and on leading-edge endeavours to take employee engagement to the next level through its commitment to employee well-being. The SAP CEO and board members see employee well-being as a strategic priority to be planned, measured and improved upon.

One of its most successful employee programmes is the SAP Global Mindfulness Practice, which started as a grassroots initiative. This movement is taken so seriously by SAP that the company even employed a Chief Mindfulness Officer to help combine emotional intelligence and neuroscience with how

---

[201] €1 = US$1.16 as on 10 October 2021.

the company addresses the concept of mindfulness, in 2012. The mindfulness programme aims to help boost self-awareness and emotional intelligence, support personal development and build resilience in the workplace. In an article written by Emma Thomasson,[202] she shared that 'providing employees with the tools and skills to decompress can flow to the bottom line'.

Since 2014, SAP has measured the impact of factors such as employee engagement, business health and culture on operating profit. The company has shown that 'staff with a better work–life balance are more resilient to stress and, therefore, more productive'.[203] Which is why, three times a year, parameters including employee engagement, business health culture index and leadership trust index are measured because the company believes that workplace culture, employee well-being and leadership trust index are tightly linked to its business success.

In fact, many of SAP's HR metrics are interwoven into its business metrics. In the *SAP Integrated Report 2020*,[204] we can see that product- and customer-related strategies are integrated with the company's people strategy, which is focused on the employee journey and lived experience.

SAP has seven strategic pillars, of which three cover the employee journey and the other four are focused on people and organizational foundation. The four organizational foundations include:

1. Drive new leadership culture

[202] Emma Thomasson, 'At Germany's SAP, Employee Mindfulness Leads to Higher Profits', Reuters, 17 May 2018, available at: https://www.reuters.com/article/us-world-work-sap-idUSKCN1II1BW. Accessed October 2021.
[203] Ibid.
[204] *SAP Integrated Report 2020*, available at: https://www.sap.com/integrated-reports/2020/en.html. Accessed October 2021.

2. Pursue the formation of an agile, entrepreneurial and innovative organization

3. Strive for inclusion and reflect the diversity of society

4. Push operational excellence and showcase human experience management solutions to customers.

And culture is the horizontal element that intertwines with all seven pillars and contributes to its business strategy and value generation.

SAP also measures the impact of its people strategy by integrating employee engagement with business success. Five out of its seven business KPIs (key performance indicators) are derived from its employee engagement survey called

Figure 9.1: SAP People Strategy

Source: SAP[205]

---

[205] SAP Integrated Report 2020, p.73 available at https://www.sap.com/integrated-reports/2020/en.html. Accessed on October 2021.

'#Unfiltered'.[206] Essentially, the #Unfiltered survey aims to strengthen employee listening and understanding, while driving managerial actions to improve employee engagement.

This transparent manner in which SAP manages employee feedback has proven very effective, as shown by the recent employee engagement index for 2020, where a high level (86 per cent) of employee engagement was reached. SAP's leadership trust net promoter score also increased to 62 per cent, while the retention rate jumped to 95.3 per cent.[207]

Dr Natalie Lotzmann, Global Head of Health and Well-Being at SAP, shared that 'there are plenty of studies showing that companies that offer programmes to promote health and well-being among their workforce are more successful than their competitors, but only very few businesses and corporate health managers present the hard facts about the financial impact of such programmes on their operating profit.'[208]

The business health culture index (BHCI) measures the general culture conditions for enabling employees to stay healthy and balanced—an indicator of the extent to which SAP offers to its employees a working environment that promotes their health and supports their long-term employability, while fostering active engagement to help SAP reach its corporate goals.[209]

The BHCI, which is obtained from the annual online employee survey, delves into the correlation between

---

[206] Ibid.

[207] Ibid.

[208] Natalie Lotzmann, 'Health and Well-Being Impact the Bottom Line—The Proof Is There!', Linkedin Pulse, 21 May 2019, available at: https://www.linkedin.com/pulse/health-well-being-impact-bottom-line-proof-dr-natalie-lotzmann/. Accessed October 2021.

[209] *SAP Integrated Report 2020*, pg 76.

employee engagement, retention and operating profit, and financial outcomes. It has also been shown to correlate with employee engagement, employee retention, CO_2 emissions and operating profit.

The 2020 BHCI was at 80 per cent.[210] As seen in the *SAP Annual Report 2020*, the BHCI has a direct impact on the people-related key performance indicators (KPIs) (Figure 9.2).

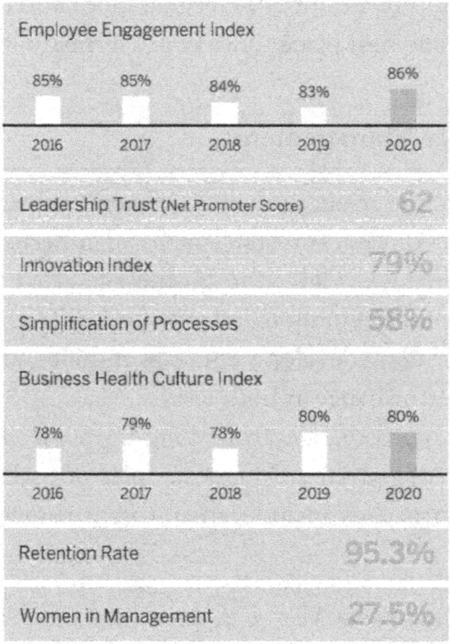

Figure 9.2: SAP's Key People-Related KPIs

Source: SAP[211]

---

[210] *SAP Annual Report 2020*, p.40, available at: https://www.sap.com/docs/download/investors/2020/sap-2020-annual-report-form-20f.pdf.   Accessed October 2021.

[211] *SAP Annual Report 2020*, p. 40.

Since 2014, SAP has been able to use enterprise data and statistical calculations to document the financial impact of the four indicators mentioned above. The BHCI was shown to have the greatest impact on operating profit and employee engagement. In an article by Jim Purcell,[212] he stated that many SAP employees love working for the company because of its supportive culture, management and well-being programmes. This assertion was supported by SAP winning Glassdoor's Best Places to Work Award for 2019.[213] Glassdoor also named SAP as the number one best place to work in Germany.

Performance Management

In addition to the science involved in measuring employee well-being, SAP also believes in establishing a high-performing culture. Thus, performance is linked to business goals at the individual and team levels. Continuous reviews and differentiated reward packages, including development opportunities, are designed to drive high performance at both levels.

These rewards range from long-term incentive plans to global share programmes. Some examples of SAP performance appraisal approaches include an initiative named 'SAP Talk',

---

[212] Jim Purcell and Steven Van Yoder (ed.), 'Case Study: SAP Shows How Employee Well-being Boosts The Bottom Line', *Forbes*, 28 October 2019, available at: https://www.forbes.com/sites/jimpurcell/2019/10/28/case-study-sap-shows-how-employee-wellbeing-boosts-the-bottom-line/. Accessed October 2021.

[213] Adam Michael Raelson, 'SAP Is Recognized Again As A Best Place to Work, According to Glassdoor 2019 Employees' Choice', *SAP Community*, 5 December 2018, available at: https://blogs.sap.com/2018/12/05/sap-is-recognized-again-as-a-best-place-to-work-according-to-glassdoor-2019-employees-choice/. Accessed October 2021.

which encourages continuous flexible dialogue. 'Move SAP' is a long-term incentive plan that rewards employees who have contributed to making a significant impact on the business.

SAP Leadership Culture

In the *SAP Integrated Report 2020*[214], we also took note of SAP fostering a strong, future-oriented leadership culture to help the company become more adaptive, innovative and collaborative. The leadership culture is centred on guiding their leaders, developing them and holding them accountable.

SAP rolled out an extended value framework that builds on 'how we run and lead' behaviours. Three new leadership behaviours, including 'unlocking potential', 'exploring possibilities', and 'making it happen together', were added to the existing five behaviours. These 'how we run and lead' behaviours ensure that there is cultural consistency and clarity for both leaders and employees.

The five existing core values are:

- Tell it like it is
- Stay curious
- Embrace differences
- Keep promises
- Build bridges

Attract, Hire and Onboard the Best Talent

Another key unique employer value proposition of SAP's is to attract people who are the right fit.

---

[214] SAP Integrated Report 2020, pg 231.

Table 9.1: How We Run Behaviours

Tell it like it is	Stay curious	Embrace differences	Keep promises	Build bridges
• Listen. Really listen. Put the facts front and centre. • Bring suggestions to the table along with opinions. • Share your point of view, discuss openly and support the outcome.	• Be willing to see change as a chance. • Innovate without fear of failure. • Be humble and never stop learning. Ideas come from everywhere.	• Create a supportive environment where everyone can be themselves. • Look for a point of view you haven't heard yet. • Try to understand where others are coming from. Trust that their intentions are positive.	• Be reliable. Say what you'll do and do what you say. • Listen with empathy to customers' challenges and goals. • Take accountability for delivering the results customers want.	• Respect expertise and execution, not just titles. • Succeed together. Fall together. No matter what. Stand up for each other. • Be willing to help and be generous with your knowledge and connections.

Source: SAP[215]

---

[215] 'Life at SAP', available at: https://www.sap.com/sea/about/careers/who-we-are/life.html. Accessed October 2021

Despite the pandemic, which saw the slowing down of recruiting activities, SAP was still able to build an inclusive workforce across the various demographics—its multi-generational workforce is accommodative of gender, disability and so on.

A total of 8,486 (12,833 in 2019) employees, or 29.4 per cent (21.4 per cent in 2019) of SAP's workforce was constituted by the 'Early Talents', or new hires with less than 2 years of postgraduate, non-professional experience. In the pool of Early Talents, 35.5 per cent (37.5 per cent in 2019) are women.[216]

As a company, SAP has continued to be a very successful talent magnet. The recruiting team works hard to position SAP as a place for future talent by working closely with approximately 3,200 universities on events, executive lectures, office visits, competitions, student club sponsorships and workshops to recruit the top students and graduates.

In 2020, more than 1,000 students were enrolled in SAP's vocational training programme in Australia, Brazil, China, Germany, Hungary, India, Ireland, Japan, New Zealand, Singapore, Switzerland and the United States. The conversion rate (number of students who joined SAP after the completion of university studies and vocational training, was 67 per cent in 2020 (and 71 per cent in 2019).[217]

SAP lives up to its name as an excellent employer with the ability to recruit and retain talent. This is evidenced by the average tenure of employees at SAP, which continues to remain high. The average tenure of employees was 7.6 years in 2020 compared to 7.3 years in 2019.[218]

---

[216] *SAP Annual Report 2020*, p. 40.

[217] Ibid.

[218] Ibid.

Even after the employees leave the company, SAP continues to stay connected with them. The SAP Alumni Network offers a programme for employees to reconnect with former colleagues while building a network of trusted SAP allies in the ecosystem. By 2020, the alumni community had grown to include 9,096 former and 4,082 current SAP employees.[219]

Future-Proofing the Workforce

Without a doubt, SAP adopts a futuristic outlook and prepares its employees to be future-ready. The stock of employee skills is reviewed periodically to ensure its currency to the rapidly changing digital economy and employees are retrained in new skills and capabilities needed for the future.

The company adopts an adaptive workforce management approach that focuses on continuous skill transformation to ensure that its employees are equipped for future work requirements.

In its robust career and growth framework, SAP personalizes this process by helping employees discover who they are, identify the areas in which they want to grow, and develop action plans to get there. While learning mainly happens on the job—through interactions with colleagues, there is also an extensive learning and development curriculum that employees can sign up for, to learn new skills. Its extensive self-paced online programmes plus training courses for technical and soft skills, are open to all employees.

SAP's peer-to-peer learning portfolio encompasses coaching, mentoring, job shadowing and facilitation opportunities. In 2020, a total of 1,007,464 courses (excluding compliance training) were signed up for by an employee base that represented 81 per cent of the company's global workforce.

---

[219] Ibid.

In Chapter 10, we covered in more depth, SAP's Fellowship Programme, which is an extension of the job shadowing programme, as well as the organization-wide reskilling programme that was implemented in its Digital Business Services (now called SAP Services) board area to prepare its global services workforce for digital transformation and success in driving intelligent enterprises in the cloud.

We caught up with Miss Renata Janini Dohmen, Global Head of Early Career Talent Attraction to delve deeper into the innovative ways that SAP uses to build a high-performing organization.

Renata Janini Dohmen
Global Head of Early Career Talent and Attraction
SAP

Question: We understand that SAP is a company that believes that employee well-being is linked to corporate success. Can you tell us the corporate philosophy supporting this thinking?
Answer: For almost fifty years, SAP has driven innovation to help the world run better and improve people's lives, and it has become one of the largest technology companies, dedicated

to customers, products, solutions and people. As SAP helps its customers innovate to run at their best; consequently, the customers can learn to solve complex problems while at the same time, address some of the world's biggest challenges.

Also, when people run at their best, they are able to change the world. With this in mind, SAP ensures that its 100,000-plus global employees run at their best with initiatives such as those that promote well-being, future-readiness and opportunities to contribute to society. Just as how SAP helps customers innovate, the company is also constantly innovating its people practices. With a highly diverse global workforce, SAP employees can also act as testbed for new market offerings.

SAP also enables its employees to use the latest and greatest technical solutions that are offered to customers. This is very empowering for the employees. As SAP utilizes the same innovation that helps its customers thrive, in its daily operations, we ourselves are also able to watch and experience the impressive evolution of the business for almost half a century—experiencing how the intelligent enterprise works while offering a safe space for people to be at their best.

Question: We know that SAP is doing very well as a company. How can it perform even better?

Answer: By ensuring that SAP continues to provide lifelong value to its customers. From the employee perspective, it means requiring our people to share a common purpose, understand the company's strategy, align their individual goals to the company's goals, lead constructively, and empower the employees to innovate and help them grow with SAP. Which is why open, relevant and timely dialogue is key.

Since the implementation of the 'how we run' behaviours, SAP has encouraged its workforce to engage regularly in quality conversations that focus on development, performance and working conditions. These conversations, also known as 'SAP Talk', have been a part of the company's culture for many years already. The 'SAP Talks' are quality dialogues for the managers and employees to connect, on at least a quarterly basis—the purpose of these dialogues is to ensure that there is regular and consistent feedback and alignment.

The 'how we run' behaviours were the result of an extensive research that was conducted together with employees around how we can be successful together and achieve the desired results. The behaviours that we desire are reflected in the interview questions used for recruiting, in 'SAP Talk' dialogues, in assessment tools, in appreciation tools, in employee communication events, in learning and development programmes and in many other opportunities for SAP to reinforce their value in driving both SAP and its employees to success.

Question: What are the different ways in which SAP measures performance?

Answer: SAP no longer uses individual performance ratings. The company has focused on continuous dialogues throughout the year so that every employee understands the company's strategy, the link between corporate and individual goals and how to achieve them. With that in mind,

- Managers have access to different business dashboards that give them visibility to progress status against key business performance indicators. Real-time data helps leaders and the different organizations take the required actions to ensure successful tracking against desired outcomes.

- Managers and employees are regularly encouraged to have continuous, forward-looking and candid 'SAP Talk' dialogues to review goals and discuss how to achieve them.
- Managers can access their Team Dashboard, where they have full visibility of real-time people-related data to make informed and objective decisions related to the employees under their charge.
- Regular conversations allow managers to better understand their employees' aspirations and needs, which in turn, help them to be better equipped to make people decisions. For example, managers have the ability to decide on short-, mid- and long-term compensation for their employees. They are also given visibility into the employees' learning and development plans, and how they are executing them. In knowing the employees well, managers can align better to the employees' professional and/or personal life stages.

Question: Can you give us some examples of the workplace culture that you measure and how it is linked to employee well-being?

Answer: We listen to employees multiple times a year to strengthen the feedback culture while creating accountability for the managers to act on the results. We listen, understand and act on employee feedback on different inter-related items to measure the status of a specific topic. These topics include the business health and culture, leadership trust, diversity and inclusion culture, innovation culture, and so on.

Employees express how they feel using statements like 'I am able to maintain a healthy balance between my work and personal life' or 'It is safe to speak up at SAP without having to worry about disfavour'.

Integral to this exercise is that the managers promote open discussions with their respective teams, along with the HR business partner or advisor, to find the best way to address the points of concern and/or to enhance the employee experience.

We have seen how this process has increased employee engagement over the years as managers adopt a laser-focused approach to drive improvements that are based on data and feedback analysis, which are reflective of employee sentiment and the relevance of the discussion.

Question: What are some of the best practices that SAP has in place to bring out the best in your leaders?

Answer: SAP constantly invests in leaders and aspiring leaders across the world. Besides the wealth of activities and programmes offered each year to cater to the diverse learning styles and development needs of its employees, the company invests in ensuring the leaders and aspiring leaders understand the evolution of the business towards the desired future state, and strives to bring the best people along for the journey.

Quarterly Leader's Communications packages, open mic sessions, 'Leaders, What's Next?' calls, co-creation workshops, along with support from dedicated Human Resources Business Partners and a clear framework on 'How We Run', an internal network of Mentors and Coaches, 'Leadership Upward Feedback' sessions and quick access to people experience and operational data, are a few examples of how SAP has equipped leaders over the years with the necessary foundation for effective leadership in the context of the business. Results of such investments are regularly measured via the leadership trust net promoter score, which promotes the identification and understanding of opportunities for further focus and, if necessary, the adjustments to be made.

Question: How do you use computational methods to link culture, employee well-being and leadership together? What are the key indices of success?

Answer: The #Unfiltered survey is part of SAP's organizational development programme that focuses on improving employee experiences by continuously listening, understanding, and acting on their feedback throughout the year. Frequent feedback gathered through the #Unfiltered surveys enable both the leaders and SAP to foster a healthy business environment for every employee.

Specifically, for leaders, the insights can help them to engage with their teams and develop action plans that address employee concerns which drive both engagement and trust in themselves and the business. It is through #Unfiltered that SAP regularly tracks key indices, such as how culture, employee well-being and leadership are linked, and how these indices help drive the success of SAP and the people who work for it.

In general terms, results are clustered into key people metrics (employee engagement and leadership trust), Organization, team and individual factors influence metrics and form key indices that the organization cares about—indices such as the business health culture index, leadership trust, diversity and inclusion, and innovation.

These results are visible on specific dashboards, which also offer other people-related data points, for example, attrition rates, completion of development plans, team composition, team financials. Thus, the dashboards provide a holistic picture to a leader. The dashboards also give leaders direct access to real-time, relevant data, coupled with the numerous offerings on people's health and wellness, growth and development, and employee engagement; thus, leaders have all the information they need to take the necessary action for the organization, team and the individual employees.

Lessons from SAP

The SAP story tells of a company that has put in place world-class people practices that are supported by a rigorous measurement system to drive a high-performing organization. It is an organization that lives and breathes its core values. And its mission is anchored by a strong corporate culture and leadership values. Its vigorous use of data to support employee and corporate performance exemplifies the powerful combination of people, data and culture.

On Glassdoor,[220] SAP has a 4.5-star rating, with 93 per cent of its employees who are willing to recommend a friend to work at SAP. Its CEO, Christian Klein, also has an approval rating of 95 per cent. SAP employees have a voice and it is heard all the way up to the top of the organization. They feel a sense of empowerment while having the flexibility to manage their work and time. In the words of the employees themselves, SAP's culture is 'second to none'.[221]

We hope that the SAP story would give you the inspiration and the ideas to embark upon the same journey to achieve corporate success through a strong corporate culture, excellence in people management and most importantly, a scientific and robust measurement system that is backed by data.

---

[220] Glassdoor Reviews, SAP, 2021, available at: https://www.glassdoor.sg/Reviews/sap-reviews-SRCH_KE0,3.htm. Accessed October 2021
[221] Ibid.

Managerial Implications

Just as how SAP has successfully transformed their organization through the clever use of data and integrated it with their culture and people measurement, we propose two questions for managers to ponder upon:

1. How do you foster a leadership culture that encourages the use of data to measure people performance?
2. With what types of people measures can you begin your analytics journey?

Chapter 10

What Got You Here Won't Get You There

There are multiple ways for organizations to get from here to there. The many future-proof approaches include continuous reskilling of employees, fostering a culture of experimentation, inculcating open innovation and practising scenario planning, as well as leveraging big data analytics.

'What got you here won't get you there'[222] is the title of one of Marshall Goldsmith's best sellers. We like this book because it shows that past successes are not good predictors for future successes.

The book is a reminder that the skills, knowledge and behaviours you have used to get to where you are today, will not be enough to get to the next level of success. While this book was written for the individual, the insights from the book can equally apply to the modern organization.

---

[222] Marshall Goldsmith, *What Got You Here Won't Get You There: How Successful People Become Even More Successful* (New York: Hyperion, 2007).

Given what got you here, won't get you there, what would it take for the modern organization to prepare for a future of success?

Impact of Technology

With technologies such as automation, AI and Internet of Things (IoT) threatening to displace workers, employers and employees alike are advised to imagine and rethink what the future of work would look like.

Technology advancement affects the higher-skilled and the lower-skilled jobs differently. In general, it tends to augment the high-skilled workers, while in contrast, tends to reduce or replace the work done by the low-skilled workers. Which is why it is estimated that 47 per cent of today's jobs, especially the lower-skilled jobs, will disappear in the next twenty-five years.[223] This translates to about 18 million jobs in India and 50 million in China.[224] And we expect this trend to exacerbate as technology advances further.

In the past year, we witnessed how quickly and expediently organizations adopted technological solutions. If not for the pandemic, experts and CEOs say that this process would have taken five years to complete.[225] When the 'Great Lockdown' was imposed across the world to curb the spread of the coronavirus, many organizations had no choice but to shift to remote and work-from-home arrangements to keep their businesses running.

---

[223] Philip Perry, '47% of Jobs Will Vanish in the Next 25 Years, Say Oxford University Researchers', Big Think, 24 December 2016, available at: https://bigthink.com/philip-perry/47-of-jobs-in-the-next-25-years-will-disappear-according-to-oxford-university. Accessed July 2021.

[224] Oliver Tonby, Li-Kai Chen and Anu Madgavkar, 'Tackling Asia's Talent Challenge: How to Adapt to a Digital Future', McKinsey, 26 July 2021, available at: https://www.mckinsey.com/featured-insights/asia-pacific/tackling-asias-talent-challenge-how-to-adapt-to-a-digital-future. Accessed September 2021.

[225] United Women Singapore, 'Distinguished Speaker Series Featuring Piyush Gupta', 11 September 2021, available at: https://uws.org.sg/distinguished-speaker-series-september-2021/. Accessed July 2021.

Many people had to master new skills and adapt to the new ways of doing work. Organizations had to introduce new tools and ways of working for employees to get work done. Managers had to learn how to manage and motivate their employees virtually.

The pandemic led many organizations to pivot their business models and accelerate the adoption of new technological solutions to reduce reliance on human beings. Manufacturing companies were seen to reconfigure their supply chains and production lines.[226] For example, the Autosphere community of automotive original equipment manufacturers (OEMs) and suppliers came together to provide global visibility of assets along the supply chain.[227] Service organizations adapted to a 'digital first' customer journey to provide contactless end-to-end operations for their customers.[228] Grab, a Singapore based company, expanded its service offerings to include rides, food, grocery and package, as well as financial and digital payment services via its mobile app.[229] Logistics organizations rolled out autonomous vehicles to replace truck drivers.[230] And we saw

---

[226] Susan Helper and Evan Soltas, 'Why the Pandemic Has Disrupted Supply Chains', The White House, 17 June 2021, available at: https://www.whitehouse.gov/cea/blog/2021/06/17/why-the-pandemic-has-disrupted-supply-chains/. Accessed October 2021.

[227] Felipe Bezamat, 'This is the Key to Manufacturing in a Post-pandemic World', World Economic Forum, 17 November 2020, available at: https://www.weforum.org/agenda/2020/11/this-is-the-key-to-manufacturing-in-a-post-pandemic-world/. Accessed October 2021.

[228] Aamer Baig, Bryce Hall, Paul Jenkins, Eric Lamarre and Brian McCarthy, 'The COVID-19 Recovery Will Be Digital: A Plan for the First 90 Days', McKinsey, 14 May 2020, available at: https://www.mckinsey.com/business-functions/mckinsey-digital/our-insights/the-covid-19-recovery-will-be-digital-a-plan-for-the-first-90-days. Accessed October 2021.

[229] Grab, 'Grab. Making Everyday Better', 2021, available at: https://www.grab.com/sg/. Accessed October 2021.

[230] Tim Dawkins, 'How COVID-19 Could Open the Door for Driverless Deliveries', World Economic Forum, 7 April 2020, available at: https://www.

retail operators leveraging sensors to control the number of people in the stores for safe distancing measures.[231]

Digital Skills

What COVID-19 has highlighted is the importance of digital skills. Digital skills are a set of skills that is no longer optional but rather, critical for the survival of organizations and for people to stay employed.

But there is a problem.

There is a huge digital skills divide in Asia Pacific, specifically in Southeast Asia. Most workers in Southeast Asia lack this important skill set because many of them are employed by small medium enterprises (SMEs). SMEs account for 99 per cent of all businesses in the region.[232] In general, SMEs have put off digitalization and digital transformation efforts and initiatives due to budget constraints and high costs. Which is why skilled knowledge workers with digital skills are in high demand—fuelled in no small part by the pandemic. The digital skills divide is not only confined to the Asia Pacific region. Over 90 per cent of executives across the world are also facing this important skills shortage.[233]

weforum.org/agenda/2020/04/how-covid-19-could-open-the-door-for-driverless-deliveries/. Accessed October 2021.

[231] Abby Kleckler, 'People Counting Technology Beyond COVID-19', Progressive Grocer, 4 May 2020, available at: https://progressivegrocer.com/people-counting-technology-beyond-covid-19. Accessed October 2021.

[232] There are more than 70 million micro-, small- and medium-sized enterprises (SMEs) in Southeast Asia, according to Michael T. Schaper, 'The Missing (Small) Businesses of Southeast Asia', Yusok Ishak Institute, No. 79, 22 July 2020, available at: https://www.iseas.edu.sg/wp-content/uploads/2020/06/ISEAS_Perspective_2020_79.pdf. Accessed September 2021.

[233] Jamilah Lim, 'What Will it Take to Bridge the Digital Skills Gap in APAC?', Techwire Asia, 25 August 2021, available at: https://techwireasia.

As more and more organizations transform their business processes to 'e-everything', from e-records, e-service, e-logistics to e-commerce, including fintech, it is expected that more and more organizations will rely on and make information technology the core of how they operate. Even traditional functions like accounting, finance, human resources, sales and marketing, and risk and compliance, will not be spared from converting to the e-way of working. Hence, the demand for digital skills will continue to grow and compound.

While the required types of digital skills will vary from country to country, it is expected that the demand for digital skills will increase by more than five-fold.[234] Up to 819 million workers are expected to have digital skills by 2025, compared to 149 million in Asia Pacific today.[235] It is also anticipated that organizations will face severe shortage in data, cloud and cybersecurity, if little is done to build up these capabilities now.

With technology becoming more and more pervasive and work becoming e-everything, it will not be a surprise to see every job changing in some way or form. Hence, learning and reskilling will be a key priority for every organization.

Skills for the Future

For organizations to thrive in this digital era, we believe that the focus on reskilling needs to go beyond digital skills. In this digitally connected economy, digital skills must function together with other skills and abilities such as strong literacy and numeracy

---

com/2021/08/what-will-it-take-to-bridge-the-digital-skills-gap-in-apac/. Accessed September 2021.

[234] Eileen Yu, 'Cloud, Data Amongst APAC Digital Skills Most Needed', *ZDNet*, 25 February 2021, available at: https://www.zdnet.com/article/cloud-data-amongst-apac-digital-skills-most-needed/. Accessed September 2021.

[235] Ibid.,

skills, critical and innovative thinking, complex problem solving, teamwork and collaboration, as well as socio-emotional skills. In other words, the focus on reskilling needs to be on both hard digital and soft cognitive and human relations skills.

Our thinking is aligned to the future of work skills as defined by the World Economic Forum.[236] Table 10.1 shows the

Table 10.1: Top Ten Skills for the Future

Top 10 Skills	Type of Skill
Analytical thinking and innovation	Problem solving
Active learning and learning strategies	Self-management
Complex problem solving	Problem solving
Critical thinking and analysis	Problem solving
Creativity, originality and initiative	Problem solving
Leadership and social influence	Working with people
Technology use, monitoring and control	Technology use and development
Technical design and programming	Technology use and development
Resilience, stress tolerance and flexibility	Self-management
Reasoning, problem solving and ideation	Problem solving

Source: Adapted from Kate Whiting, 'These are the top 10 job skills of tomorrow'.

top ten skills that the World Economic Forum believes would become critical for work in the future.

Other than the skills highlighted above, design is another important skill because:

---

[236] Kate Whiting, "These are the top 10 job skills of tomorrow—and how long it takes to learn them", World Economic Forum, October 21, 2020, https://www.weforum.org/agenda/2020/10/top-10-work-skills-of-tomorrow-how-long-it-takes-to-learn-them/, accessed September 2021.

- Design can provide differentiation in customer experiences and create an emotional connection between a brand and its customers.
- It is essential for innovation, specifically when design-thinking skills are applied to systematically extract, learn and adopt human-centred techniques to solve problems in a creative and innovative way.

Recognizing the importance of design skills, Indra Nooyi, the former president and CEO of PepsiCo, created a new executive role—Chief Design Officer—to oversee design-led innovations across all of PepsiCo's brands.[237] The focus on design at PepsiCo goes beyond the aesthetics and the design of the products, it is also about creating experiences that are meaningful and relevant.

Reskilling Approaches

Given that time will wait for no man, or in this case, no organization, how can organizations reskill their employees quickly and expediently? What innovative approaches can organizations adopt to expedite this reskilling process?

There are many reskilling approaches that are available and widely practised. We would like to offer the following approaches for organizations to consider and adopt as part of their reskilling efforts:

- Annual mandatory training
- Contextualized and integrated models of training
- Credentialled training

---

[237] James de Vries, 'PepsiCo's Chief Design Officer on Creating an Organization Where Design Can Thrive', *Harvard Business Review*, 11 August 2015, available at: https://hbr.org/2015/08/pepsicos-chief-design-officer-on-creating-an-organization-where-design-can-thrive. Accessed September 2021.

- Learning from leaders
- Peer learning
- Self-paced learning
- Immersive training
- Company-wide training
- Learning from leading companies

The one unique approach that we would like to highlight is the 'learning from leading companies' approach. This approach, which was launched in January 2021, was made possible through public–private partnership.

At the beginning of this year, SkillsFuture Singapore, a national reskilling organization that was established by the Singapore Government to foster and inculcate a mindset of continuous learning,[238] introduced the Queen Bee[239] programme to facilitate leading companies in championing skills development for companies in the same industry or sector.

The primary objective of this programme is to help the SMEs accelerate their reskilling and transform their businesses. Twenty-two Queen Bee companies[240] have been selected by SkillsFuture to provide advice on skills, as well as guide the participating organizations to identify and acquire skills needed for business transformation. Some Queen Bee companies go one step further by providing traineeships to the SMEs.

Table 10.2 describes the different reskilling approaches that are commonly practised in leading organizations, in more detail.

---

[238] 'About SkillsFuture', SkillsFuture SG, 6 August 2021, available at: https://www.skillsfuture.gov.sg/AboutSkillsFuture. Accessed September 2021.

[239] '"Queen Bee" Firms to Mobilise Other Employers to Uplift Their Sectors' Capabilities: Lawrence Wong', *Channel News Asia*, 21 January 2021, available at: https://www.channelnewsasia.com/business/singapore-industry-workforce-lawrence-wong-skillsfuture-423231. Accessed September 2021.

[240] Ibid.

Table 10.2: Different Reskilling Approaches

Reskilling Approach	Description
Annual Mandatory Training	All major technology companies, including Cisco Systems, Dell and Microsoft, require all their employees to complete mandatory curricula that are aligned to the companies' annual fiscal strategies. The courses are administered using a combination of kick-off meetings and e-learning courses.
	The kick-off meetings are often in-person events for employees to interact directly with the executive leadership team. Following the plenary sessions, break-out sessions are held to impart relevant and role-specific courses. However, due to the pandemic, most kick-off meetings have been moved online.
Contextualized Model of Training	The contextualized model of learning has been widely used to drive reskilling in digital skills. This model leverages real-world materials and contexts, and is typically instructor-led. For example, the instructor might help construction workers practice using a blueprint technology application that is widely used by general contractors.
Integrated Models of Training	The integrated model combines instruction in foundational skills (literacy, numeracy, digital skills and spoken English) with simultaneous training

	for a specific occupation or industry. For example, the training instructor might help workers learn digital skills as part of the process for becoming a telehealth coordinator or medical assistant.
Credentialled Training	Credentialled training has become popular in recent times as a way for organizations to measure skill-level proficiency. For example, in 2016, L'Oreal partnered with General Assembly to implement a new assessment—the Certified Marketer Level 1, to measure required marketing skills in the digital economy.[241] Another example comes from OCBC. Given the importance of data analytics, the bank rolled out the OCBC's Data Certification Pathway Course[242] to increase proficiency levels in programming and coding, data governance, data storytelling and visualization, data computation and modelling, and data mining.

[241] Erica Sweeney, 'L'Oréal, General Assembly Create New Assessment for Digital Marketers', Marketing Dive, 13 November 2018, *available at: https://www.marketingdive.com/news/loreal-general-assembly-create-new-assessment-for-digital-marketers/542071/.* Accessed September 2021.

[242] OCBC Bank, 'OCBC Bank Launches Digital Transformation Programme For 29,000 Employees', Fintech Singapore, 8 May 2018, available at: https://fintechnews.sg/19664/fintech/ocbc-bank-digital-transformation-programme-for-29000-employees/. Accessed June 2021.

Table 10.2: (Continued)

Reskilling Approach	Description
	At SUTD Academy (Singapore University of Technology and Design Academy), several streams of credentialled training, including Digital HR, have been rolled out to help organizations reskill their employees.
Learning from Leaders	Another noticeable reskilling trend is for leaders to impart their knowledge, skills and experiences to employees through scheduled programmes that are conducted on a monthly or a quarterly basis.

At SAP, 'Flyback Friday' sessions were held once a quarter for leaders to coach employees to be better services consultants and technical account managers. These learning sessions were conducted via Microsoft Teams and they included lectures, hands-on activities, quizzes and presentations. Each quarterly training topic was carefully chosen to focus on the skills that needed development. Examples of topics that were selected included 'diffusing escalations' and 'commercial management'.[243] |

---

[243] Based on insights from Jovina Ang's work and consulting engagements at SAP.

I[244] have also rolled out this type of learning initiative at Microsoft. 'The Year of the Manager' was held on a monthly basis for managers to learn firsthand from the executive team. Friday Forum was another technical learning initiative to impart new insights on new technologies and share best practices from across the world.

The '10 Cups of Coffee' programme was another that I launched to promote informal learning between leaders and employees. As the name of the programme suggests, employees can book a session with leaders on the executive team over a cup of coffee.

Leaders can also develop employees through mentoring. The mentor–mentee relationship can significantly enhance development, especially at the early- and mid-career stages. To ensure a successful mentoring relationship, typically, HR would prepare a set of mentoring resources, as well as set guidelines to define its goals.

Job shadowing allows employees to learn through observation. It can help employees gain new expertise and multidimensional problem-solving skills. In general, job shadowing is offered to high-potential employees for them to learn from leaders.

(Continued)

[244] 'I' here refers to Jovina Ang.

Table 10.2: (Continued)

Reskilling Approach	Description
Peer Learning	Peer learning is a form of collaborative learning that has been proven to work for adults. There are several benefits of peer learning, including developing feedback loops, communication skills, professional development, teamwork and collaboration, as well as building a stronger company culture through peer interactions. It is easy to implement—leaders can facilitate peer learning by getting employees to share their work in team meetings or assign teams of employees to solve problems. The Motorola Total Customer Satisfaction (TCS) initiative was an initiative that encouraged peer learning. Different employees were brought together to share ideas and solve quality issues. Even though this was a formal corporate initiative, participation in the TCS initiative was totally voluntary. The TCS initiative was estimated to save Motorola over US$2.2 billion per annum.[245]

[245] Barnaby J. Feder, 'At Motorola, Quality Is a Team Sport', The New York Times, 21 January, 1993, available at: https://www.nytimes.com/1993/01/21/business/at-motorola-quality-is-a-team-sport.html. Accessed September 2021.

Another successful peer learning programme is Seth Godin's altMBA[246] programme. The programme costs US$4,450 to participate in. Unlike the typical MBA, the altMBA is a peer- and community-based leadership and management programme that runs for thirty-one days. The programme is completely delivered online and focuses on 'learning by doing'. Learning is enhanced through teamwork, personalized feedback, coaching, curated readings and the delivery of thirteen projects in four weeks.

Each session of the altMBA workshop is led by a group of coaches who help the participants in their individual and group work. There are no assigned teachers or professors for the course, even Seth Godin himself does not personally teach any modules of the course. The coaches play the primary role of nudging the participants toward their goals. The participants are expected to work in small groups and openly critique one another's work to learn and grow.

---

[246] For more information on the altMBA programme, please see: https://altmba.com/faq#what-is-the-curriculum. Accessed September 2021.

(Continued)

Table 10.2: (Continued)

Reskilling Approach	Description
Self-Paced Learning	While organizations can design a rich set of learning experiences on the job, they can also enable employees to continuously train and educate themselves. This learning approach is gaining traction as more and more employees recognize that 'the learning curve is the earning curve'[247].
	MOOCs (massive open online courses) provide a platform for self-paced learning. The popular MOOCs include Coursera, edX, FutureLearn, Khan Academy and Udemy. People are also getting more comfortable in learning on MOOCs, as shown by their widespread adoption and advanced video learning, which has more than doubled since 2015.[248]
	There are five main benefits for organizations to offer self-paced learning: • **Efficiency**: With self-pacing, each employee can make best use of his or her time to meet their learning objectives.

---

[247] Josh Bersin, 'New Research Shows Why Focus On Teams, Not Just Leaders, Is Key To Business Performance', Forbes, 3 March 2016, available at: https://www.forbes.com/sites/joshbersin/2016/03/03/why-a-focus-on-teams-not-just-leaders-is-the-secret-to-business-performance/?sh=77eab05f24d5. Accessed September 2021.

[248] Ibid.

	• **Effectiveness**: An interesting study by Jonathan G. Tullis and Aaron S. Benjamin[249] found that self-paced learning can improve memory performance. • **Convenience**: Employees can schedule learning based on his or her own schedules and preferences. • **Scalability**: The investment cost is front-end-loaded. Organizations can train as many people as necessary with modest incremental costs • **Reusability**: With minimal investment, organizations can retrain employees to fight 'skills decay'.
Immersive Training	While reskilling programmes are necessary for employees to acquire new skills, more effort needs to be devoted to institutionalizing 'learning by doing' for employees to internalize and practise what they have learned. In so doing, employees can develop what Herminia Ibarra has called 'outsight',[250] which is insight that can only be acquired through doing and taking action.

(Continued)

[249] Jonathan G. Tullis, and Aaron S. Benjamin, 'On the Effectiveness of Learning', J Mem Lang, 64, no.2, 1 February 2011, p.109–188. Available at: 10.1016/j.jml.2010.11.002. Accessed September 2021.
[250] Herminia Ibarra, Act Like a Leader, Think Like a Leader (Boston: *Harvard Business Review Press, 2015*), p.4.

Table 10.2: (Continued)

Reskilling Approach	Description
	According to Herminia Ibarra, plunging into new projects and activities, interacting with different kinds of people and experimenting with unfamiliar ways of getting things done provides an experiential learning that cannot be achieved through classroom or e-learning.
	The SAP Fellowship Programme[251] is an extension of the job shadowing programme which provides outsight for learning and development in a completely new discipline or area. Any full-time employee can sign up for the SAP fellowship to learn a new skill, explore a new career path or learn how to manage a function in a different department in a different country.
	This unique programme provides an opportunity for employees to gain experience and exposure. Through this programme, employees can get outside their comfort zones, try new things, and still do great work for SAP. It also helps employees build new personal and professional networks.

[251] Suvarna Kartha, 'SAP Labs India—Indeed, A Great Place to Work!—My Story', LinkedIn, 21 August 2019, available at: https://www.linkedin.com/pulse/sap-labs-india-indeed-great-place-work-my-story-suvarna-kartha-1d. Accessed September 2021.

Company-wide Reskilling	Instead of rolling out a piece-meal approach to training, some companies have adopted a company-wide approach to reskilling as an investment for the future, so that all the employees can reap the benefits of a consistent training curriculum for their learning and development.
	PricewaterhouseCoopers (PwC) has committed an investment of US$3 billion into the New World, New Skills programme[252] to reskill its 276,000 employees in five reskilling building blocks. The reskilling blocks included curated classroom and virtual training on data visualization, data analytics and automation, and the use of the 'Digital Fitness for the World' app to measure employees' 'Digital Fitness Score'. This score endowed them with the ability to recommend customized upskilling plans for score improvement. There were also a series of e-learning courses offered on PwC's learning platform; participation in designing solutions and innovation on the company's collaboration platform; as well as an accelerated programme designed for employees with advanced digital skills to automate process and improve user experience across the company.[253]

[252] Amanda Bergson-Shilcock, "Boosting Digital Literacy in the Workplace", National Skills Coalition, December 15, 2020, https://www.nationalskillscoalition.org/wp-content/uploads/2021/01/12152020-NSC-Boosting-Digital-Literacy.pdf, accessed September 2021.

[253] Price Waterhouse Coopers (PwC), "New World New Skills", 2020, https://www.pwc.com/sg/en/publications/new-world-new-skills.html, accessed September 2021.

Table 10.2: (Continued)

Reskilling Approach	Description
	OCBC Bank has committed S$30 million in the 'Future Smart Programme' to reskill its 29,000 employees over a period of three years. The first part of the training programme, which was rolled out in 2018, focused on digital transformation and digital skills.[254] Recently, the programme was expanded to include sustainability and environmental, social and governance (ESG) topics.[255] SAP started its organization-wide reskilling effort in 2017[256] when the company shifted its product portfolio towards digital innovation and cloud computing. The organization-wide reskilling was driven by the Digital Business Services division (now called SAP Services). It included a sequence of learning journeys, comprising boot camps, job shadowing, peer coaching and digital learning, to prepare the services employees transition from a technical role to a more customer advisory and consultative role.

[254] OCBC Bank, "OCBC Bank Launches the Largest Workforce Digital Transformation Programme for 29,000 employees", May 8, 2018, https://www.ocbc.com/group/media/release/2018/ocbc-future-smart-programme.page, accessed September 2021.
[255] Natalie Choy, "OCBC Rolls Out Sustainability Training for Staff as Part of S$30m Skills Drive", Banking and Finance, July 8, 2021, https://www.businesstimes.com.sg/banking-finance/ocbc-rolls-out-sustainability-training-for-staff-as-part-of-s30m-skills-drive, accessed September 2021.
[256] Peter Gumbel, and Angelika Reich, "Building the Workforce of Tomorrow, Today", McKinsey Quarterly, https://www.mckinsey.com/business-functions/organization/our-insights/building-the-workforce-of-tomorrow-today, accessed September 2021.

	SAP also developed a strategic training plan and mapped each employee comparing his or her current skills to the required future skills in the next five years, twenty years and even thirty years.
Learning from Leading Companies	As mentioned above, this unique learning approach resulted from a public–private partnership. Twenty-two leading companies, including KornFerry, Google, Microsoft, Prudential and Shopee, have signed up as Queen Bee companies to help transform their respective industries and sectors. These companies have committed to work with SMEs over the course of the year to help them identify skill gaps and support them in their skills development. For example, Shopee, a leading e-commerce platform in Southeast Asia and Taiwan, has allocated a skills manager who will plan, source, design and implement a training plan that is tailored to each of the participating SMEs.[257] Other than providing this service, Shopee has also committed to creating a skills support ecosystem for the SME sellers to learn and build the necessary capability for excelling in e-commerce.

[257] Yong Hui Ting, "Shopee to Help SMEs Upskill via SkillsFuture Queen Bee Programme", The Business Times, March 31, 2021, https://www.businesstimes.com.sg/sme/shopee-to-help-smes-upskill-via-skillsfuture-queen-bee-programme, accessed September 2021.

Building a Culture of Experimentation

Other than adopting the multiple reskilling approaches highlighted above, some organizations have turned to experimentations to reskill and drive innovation.

Bookings.com is a company that has fostered experimentation in its culture. It is estimated that Bookings.com runs more than 1,000 experiments simultaneously and up to 25,000 experiments per year to enhance the search and booking experience for its customers.[258] Despite the low success rate of its experiments, which is estimated at 10 per cent,[259] the website has been able to learn from these failures to course correct, eliminate unfavourable options and hone and focus on more promising alternatives to drive growth for its business. For example, they ran a bold experiment during the peak holiday season in December 2017.[260] Instead of displaying the usual long list of options to customers, they presented only three options: 'accommodations', 'flights' and 'rental cars', when customers searched for holiday options in any city that they were thinking of vacationing in.

At Google, '20 per cent Time' was introduced to allow employees to work on side projects in areas that were of interest to them. Many key products such as Google News, Google Maps, Gmail and Adsense are the results of such side projects.[261] While this practice has since been abandoned,

---

[258] Stefan Thomke, "Building a Culture of Experimentation", Harvard Business Review, March-April 2020, https://hbr.org/2020/03/building-a-culture-of-experimentation, accessed September 2021.

[259] Ibid.

[260] Ibid.

[261] Jillian D'Onfro, "The Truth About Google's Famous '20% Time' Policy", Business Insider, April 18, 2015, https://www.businessinsider.com/

Google still does experimentation, but in a more concerted and focused way. Before any manager can approve any 20-per cent projects, they are first judged by how productive their teams are. Additionally, Google has established the Google X Lab to focus and drive experimentation and innovation efforts within the organization.[262]

Another example comes from Atlassian, an Australian software company that was established in 2002.[263] The company fosters a culture of experimentation in a structured format because the founders and co-CEOs believe that 'structured and constrained innovation' is a way to drive creativity.

The teams of employees can practise different forms of structured innovation, from 20 per cent time (1 day a week) to practising experimentation in the Innovation Week, which is held after every five weeks. Every quarter, the 'ShipIt' hackathon is held to provide a space for employees to drop what they are doing and collaborate with one another, often with ad hoc teams, to pursue wild ideas and look at new ways of thinking about the problem.[264] Additionally, the company has introduced games or what it calls 'plays' to encourage teamwork and collaboration across the whole organization.

Many Asian organizations have also jumped on the experimentation bandwagon. Hackathons are a popular approach

google-20-per cent-time-policy-2015-4, accessed September 2021.

[262] Christopher Mims, "The '20% Time' Perk at Google Is No More", The Atlantic, August 16, 2013, https://www.theatlantic.com/technology/archive/2013/08/20-time-perk-google-no-more/312063/, accessed September 2021.

[263] Atlassian, "Who We are", 2021, https://www.atlassian.com/company, accessed September 2021.

[264] Dominic Price, "What is a Culture of Innovation?", Inside Atlassian, April 7, 2019, https://www.atlassian.com/blog/inside-atlassian/how-to-build-culture-of-innovation-every-day, accessed September 2021.

to garner new ideas and ways of thinking from outside the organization. In 2017, AirAsia launched its inaugural Airvolution Hackathon with the objective to create new applications and tools for the airline to further differentiate itself.[265] When he was interviewed about the Airvolution Hackathon, Tony Fernandes, Group CEO of AirAsia, commented:

> 'We still have a lot of things we can do to improve our business by bringing in digital. I still don't know if a Hackathon is the best way to go; I'm in the process of testing it out. But based on the question, "How can we collect many ideas and move forward as quickly as possible?" this is my way to put ourselves on the fast track to generating plenty of intellectual property and creative ideas for the company—and also to forge a relationship with all 100 participants today.'[266]

DBS Bank, one of the pioneer banks in Singapore and one of the top global banks, runs all kinds of hackathons across the organizations for its employees of all ranks, from juniors to senior executives. Instead of sending its talents to 'fancy business schools', DBS puts them through the hackathon experience to develop new skills and ways of thinking. As explained by Piyush Gupta, CEO of DBS Bank,

---

[265] 'Coming soon: AirAsia's First Ever Airvolution Hackathon!', AirAsia, 16 January 2017, available at: https://ir.airasia.com/news.html/id/627977. Accessed September 2021.

[266] TechSauce, 'Tony Fernandes Talks AirAsia's Digital Arline Roadmap for 2017, Upcoming CVC & Accelerator', 19 March 2017, available at: https://techsauce.co/tech-and-biz/tony-fernandes-talks-airasia-digital-airline-roadmap-2017. Accessed September 2021.

'We run all kinds of hackathons. We run twenty or twenty-five of them. We have forty- and fifty-year-olds who work with kids in their twenties to spend five days in a warehouse and come up with an app. The excitement people have when they come up with an app to solve a trivial problem is massive. But, it is all about changing people's mindsets. And the confidence to know they can actually do things that make an impact and the way work progresses.'[267]

James Dyson, the billionaire entrepreneur who founded Dyson Ltd, encourages the experimental mindset in his organization by encouraging his employees to ask silly questions. With the world changing so fast, he says past experience is of little value. Rather, he believes:

'Knowing what has worked in the past really doesn't help you at all now. In fact, it always does the opposite. It's a hindrance . . . I don't mind silly suggestions, in fact, I encourage them. I think naive curiosity, naive questioning, wrong suggestions are good ideas. An experienced person will only put forward a sensible suggestion, which might work, whereas a naive person, or a young person who is unafraid to make mistakes, will ask the wrong question, will make an outrageous suggestion, which might actually be a very good idea.'[268]

---

[267] Nik Gowing and Chris Langdon, 'The New GANDALF: "How to Ensure the Switch Goes On"', *Thinking the Unthinkable* (Woodbridge: John Catt Educational Ltd, 2018), available at: https://www.thinkunthink.org/perch/resources/documents/ttudbsbankchapter.pdf. Accessed September 2021.
[268] Sumiko Tan, 'Lunch With Sumiko: No such thing as a silly idea, says billionaire inventor James Dyson', *The Straits Times*, 5 September 2021, available at: https://www.straitstimes.com/singapore/lunch-with-sumiko-

Embracing Open Innovation

Open innovation provides a collaborative way for organizations to future-proof themselves and innovate beyond the traditional confines of the organization. It is a relatively new concept and a paradigm shift from the 'old school' way of thinking about innovation, which is centred on the concept of closed innovation, where research and development (R&D) is invested in driving innovation within the organization. In contrast, open innovation allows ideas to be generated from within the organization, as well as externally. And these ideas can come from multiple sources.

The term 'open innovation' was first introduced by Henry Chesbrough[269] to describe a situation where an organization uses multiple external sources, such as customer feedback, published patents, competitors, external agencies, the public, as well as its own internal knowledge, sources and resources, such as staff or R&D, for driving innovation in its products, services, business models, processes and so on. Conceptually, open innovation is a more distributed, more participatory, more decentralized approach to innovation. Henry Chesbrough described open innovation as, 'the use of purposive inflows and outflows of knowledge to accelerate internal innovation, and expand the markets for external use of innovation, respectively.'[270]

---

no-such-thing-as-a-silly-idea-says-billionaire-inventor-james-dyson. Accessed September 2021.

[269] Henry Chesbrough and Marcel Bogers, 'Explicating Open Innovation: Clarifying an Emerging Paradigm for Understanding Innovation', in In Henry Chesbrough, Wim Vanhaverbeke, and Joel West (Eds.), *New Frontiers in Open Innovation*, (Oxford: Oxford University Press, 2014), pp. 3–28.

[270] Henry Chesbrough, 'Everything You Need to Know about Open Innovation', *Forbes*, 11 March 2011, available at: https://www.forbes.com/sites/henrychesbrough/2011/03/21/everything-you-need-to-know-about-open-innovation/. Accessed September 2021.

Useful knowledge has become widespread and can come from a diverse number of industries and sectors. The shift towards open innovation offers novel ways to create value for an organization. Open innovation can reduce costs, accelerate time to market, increase differentiation in the market, as well as create new revenue streams for the company. Which is why the logic for using only an internally oriented, centralized approach to R&D, is becoming obsolete. Furthermore, open innovation can provide a learning opportunity for employees to acquire new skills from outside the organization.

Moët Hennessy Louis Vuitton, or commonly known as LVMH, a leading French house of luxury goods, is a company that has been practising open innovation for many years. The company's innovation strategy is centred on open innovation, a collaborative and outward-looking co-creation approach that seeks to exploit the fact that vast volumes of knowledge exist outside the research centres of companies. Every year, LVMH hosts several innovation events and gives out several innovation awards.

In 2017, LVMH launched 'La Maison des Startups' to accelerate collaboration between startups and its seventy maisons.[271] Every year, fifty startups with innovations that can benefit LVMH are selected and given access to the Station F campus in Paris. The programme's distinctive multi-sector approach enables maisons to engage with entrepreneurs whose innovations are relevant to the different LVMH business groups—wines and spirits, fashion and leather goods, perfumes

---

[271] 'Startup Day at La Maison des Startups LVMH at Station F Accelerates Collaboration between LVMH Maisons and New Tech Businesses', LVMH, 9 December 2019, available at: https://www.lvmh.com/news-documents/news/startup-day-at-la-maison-des-startups-lvmh-at-station-f-accelerates-collaboration-between-lvmh-maisons-and-new-tech-businesses/. Accessed September 2021.

and cosmetics, watches and jewellery, and selective retailing. The programme is wide-ranging and LVMH selects startups with unique approaches to branding and using sustainable raw materials, to be a part of the programme. LVMH has also selected startups with innovations involving the use of data and application of AI to improve its supply chain and operations.

While knowledge and skills are transferred from LVMH to the startups, the reverse has also taken place, with learning flowing from the startups to LVMH. For example, one of the startups, Alcméon, brought new social messaging skills to LVMH to address the increasing number of consumer requests on social media and instant messaging. Alcméon developed a tool combining AI, supervised chatbots and human touch for LVMH.[272]

Open innovation is not only a concept that applies to big companies. Small companies, SMEs and even hawkers can adopt the open innovation concept to innovate and transform their business processes.

A good example of open innovation in a small enterprise can be seen in Lao Hung Jia, a chicken rice hawker stall in Singapore. In order to innovate, the hawker stall worked with the Food Innovation and Resource Centre (FIRC) at the Singapore Polytechnic, to simplify the food production process by developing pre-mixed and pre-packaged sauces to prepare the accompanying chilli sauce, chicken broth and sweet soya sauce for the chicken rice dish.[273] The FIRC thus brought open

---

[272] Station F at LVMH, 'New at STATION F! Meet LVMH's LuxuryTech Startups', *Medium*, 19 April 2018, available at: https://medium.com/station-f/new-at-station-f-meet-lvmhs-luxurytech-startups-b4fc5136241e.   Accessed September 2021.

[273] Pascale Crama, Chon Phung Lim, Cintia Kulzer Sacilotto and Jovina Ang, 'Innovating Singapore's Chicken Rice', Teaching Note: Singapore Management University, SMU-20-0050, February 2021.

innovation to Lao Hung Jia by developing pre-mixed and pre-packaged sauces for the hawker.

Scenario Planning

Another way to drive innovation is to adopt scenario planning. Scenario planning is a strategic planning method that was popularized by Shell.[274] We believe scenario planning is a valuable method for organizations to manage uncertainties, plan for the future and 'get there'.

The intent of the scenarios is to help leaders gain clarity and open their minds to the new dynamics of the future, while providing an intuitive understanding of the world that precedes and frames analytical understanding. By conducting scenario planning, leaders can identify a range of possible outcomes, evaluate the impacts and consequently, manage both positive and negative possible outcomes. Hence, it is a strategic planning method that calls for proactive management in the future.

By building organizational awareness of what could happen, it is more likely for leaders to spot warning signs of 'brewing' and unexpected challenges, and respond accordingly. It can also define the set of assumptions about potential business realities and ensuing outcomes. Additionally, scenario planning can help organizations be agile and adaptive to the multiple outcomes that might occur. For example, should a worst-case event arise, scenario planning can add tremendous value by listing out the multiple outcomes and detailing the steps needed to contain the damage. Conversely, it can be equally advantageous for best-case scenarios, especially to help organizations drive the appropriate

---

[274] Angela Wilkinson and Roland Kupers, 'Living in the Futures', *Harvard Business Review*, May 2013, https://hbr.org/2013/05/living-in-the-futures. Accessed September 2021.

actions, for example, to capture market share, should a product line become hugely successful.

Since the 1970s, Shell has been developing possible 'visions' of the future by asking what-if questions to consider events that have even the remotest possibilities of occurring to stretch the bounds of thinking of its leadership team. Scenario planning has helped Shell visualize plausible and challenging descriptions of the future that the company might face. It has also helped them tackle the tougher energy and environmental issues.[275] For example, Shell developed the 'World Energy Model' by leveraging six key drivers of data of the energy system, specifically, population, economic growth, environmental pressures, technology, resource availability and consumers, to understand how these drivers impact the evolution of energy demand in different countries and sectors.[276]

Scenario planning is a strategic planning method that encompasses three broad steps:

- Defining the current reality for the organization and wider world, and envisioning how it might be different in future.
- Considering the different scenarios and what the differences in scenarios would mean for the organization.
- Building a nimble response strategy that is based on the new knowledge, which might include developing a plan, mitigating a risk or exploring an opportunity.

While working for Motorola, many years ago, I[277] teamed up with key leaders from across the world, to adopt scenario planning to envision how the market of two-way radios might evolve.

---

[275] 'What are Shell Scenarios?', Shell, n.d.m., available at: https://www.shell.com/energy-and-innovation/the-energy-future/scenarios/what-are-scenarios.html. Accessed September 2021.

[276] Ibid.

[277] 'I' refers to Jovina Ang here.

Several workshops were held with multiple stakeholders across the world to envision the many applications for the two-way radio. These workshops led to the introduction of several new product lines and solutions to address new market applications, such as enhancing customer service, coordinating manufacturing lines, addressing recreation needs, such as camping, and so on.

Big Data Analytics

There is so much data that is collected every day by the various communication devices that we use. Every swipe of the phone, every click of a button and every post on social media generate data that organizations can collect easily. These types of data, which are known as big data, comprise the enormous amount of data that is collected every second by organizations for reasons such as understanding consumer behaviour and preferences, employee sentiments and level of engagement. By 2025, it is predicted that there will be 175 zettabytes (10^{21}) of data.[278] Without a doubt, big data analytics provide a way for organizations to get 'from here to there'.

Given the growing importance of big data for organizational success, what exactly is big data? To expand upon this concept, we would like to borrow Hannah Fry's[279] definition. Fry has defined big data using the acronym 'DATA'. 'D' stands for dimensions because of its many dimensions. 'A' stands for automatic, because such data is collected automatically. 'T' stands for time, as in real-

---

[278] 'Digital Transformation Series: Satya Nadella on Digital Transformation for Microsoft'[video], YouTube, posted by Centre of Executive Education, 28 July 2020, available at: https://www.youtube.com/watch?v=_zgSSeZJH30. Accessed March 2021.

[279] 'Big Data', *The Infinite Monkey Cage with Brian Cox and Robin Ince* [podcast], *BBC* Series 18, 16 July 2018, available at: https://www.bbc.co.uk/programmes/b0b9wbf8. Accessed July 2021.

time. And the second 'A' stands for AI—the critical technology that is used for the collection of big data.

Without a doubt, the constant stream of data can provide valuable insights for organizations to create new growth opportunities, build customer loyalty, drive efficiency improvements, as well as provide opportunities for better decision-making and organization reinvention. Data can also help organizations run their businesses better. Netflix is an example of a company that has leveraged big data to drive its investment decisions, as well as define its growth strategy. Netflix's rise from a DVD-rental service to the world's most valuable media company is powered by big data analytics.

Thanks to big data, the company was able to understand its subscribers' preferences and tailor unique viewing experiences for each user. It is believed that the same algorithms that helped Netflix with content curation, are also helping it with content production and marketing. Its successful TV shows and movies such as *House of Cards*, *Orange Is The New Black*, and *Birdbox* have attracted a lot of attention and high viewership, while driving up subscription rates.[280] Its success with big data boasts a 93 per cent customer retention rate, compared to Amazon Prime's 75 per cent and Hulu's 64 per cent.[281]

To provide personalized service to each of its subscribers, Netflix collects big data from every subscriber to build models to analyze customer behaviour and buying patterns. It collects detailed customer interaction and response data to a TV show or movie, including the time and date logged in to watch a show, the device used, whether the show was paused or fast

---

[280] Michael Dixon, 'How Netflix Used Big Data and Analytics to Generate Billions', Selerity, April 5, 2019, available at: https://seleritysas.com/blog/2019/04/05/how-netflix-used-big-data-and-analytics-to-generate-billions. Accessed July 2021.
[281] Ibid.

forwarded, and the total time taken to finish watching the show. The company also takes screenshots of the scenes that are watched repeatedly.

Big data is also used by luxury brands such as LVMH, to provide personalized and unique one-in-a-million experiences to their customers, so that every customer feels special and attended to. Additionally, luxury brands also use big data to maximize the return on marketing spend by understanding customers' various touch points along their customer journey. In so doing, the luxury brands are able to effectively apportion marketing spend across the different channels, while minimizing cannibalization between the different sales channels, for example, reduction of sales in the physical stores due to the introduction of LVMH online stores.

But big data is not only for helping organizations improve personalization and offer better customer experiences, it is also about helping organizations make their assets perform better. At General Electric, big data is used to optimize machine performance. For example, to improve performance of wind turbines to produce up to 10 per cent more energy from the same amount of wind.[282] At AIG, big data is used to create a culture and environment where employees can thrive and play a part in driving the company's strategy.[283] At Geckos, big data is used to conduct remote organizational network analysis to improve employee experience.[284]

---

[282] 'How Companies are Using Big Data and Analytics', McKinsey, 21 April 2016, available at: https://www.mckinsey.com/business-functions/mckinsey-analytics/our-insights/how-companies-are-using-big-data-and-analytics. Accessed September 2021.

[283] Ibid.

[284] Expert Panel of the Forbes Human Resources Council, '15 Effective Ways HR Teams Can Leverage Big Data', Forbes, 2 February 2021, available at: https://www.forbes.com/sites/forbeshumanresourcescounc

Managerial Implications

The phrase 'what got you here, won't get you there' is a reminder for organizations to not be complacent—leaders and managers need to take a hard look at their methods and envision what the future looks like, and then work backwards to ascertain what is needed to get there. We also encourage them to develop plausible future scenarios to visualize future outcomes.

While there are many reskilling approaches, as well as many future-proof methods that are available, including experimentation, open innovation, scenario planning and big data analytics, the approach you choose for your organization needs to take into consideration its people, culture and data-savviness at present.

Regardless of the approach you choose for preparing the organization to 'get there', you will also need to measure your progress. Data informs us how we are doing and provides information on how well or how badly we are progressing. And quite honestly, in practice, if you can't measure it, you can't improve it.

It is also equally important to select the correct measures to show the impact of the different reskilling and future-proofing approaches. Hence, to determine which measures of data are useful, it is important to consider cause and effect, rather than just look at short-term measures, such as the evaluations of training programmes.

il/2021/02/02/15-effective-ways-hr-teams-can-leverage-big-data/. Accessed September 2021.

Chapter 11

Looking Through the Future Lens

As there is no crystal ball to predict the future of work, adaptability and agility will be key for addressing the many challenges that emerge from the confluence of disruptive forces.

A discussion about how the modern organization could look through the future lens will not be complete without examining the major forces that are disrupting the world of work. There is a confluence of four disruptive forces at play when it comes to the world of work, including demographic imbalances, geopolitics, technology and economic contraction.

As these forces gather steam, they will make the world of work even more VUCA (volatile, uncertain, complex and ambiguous). Hence, there will be implications as to how the modern organization will transform itself by managing critical factors, such as people, culture and data.

Which is why the modern organization needs to constantly learn from its failures, course correct, change direction, as well as make tweaks to capitalize on the growth opportunities. In other words, adopt a judicious malleability mindset.

Demographic Imbalances

In today's world, there exist demographic imbalances that differentiate the more developed countries from the developing countries.[285] On one hand, we have an ageing population in the more developed countries, whereas on the other hand, a younger population in the developing countries. The population in the developed countries is ageing rapidly. This trend is most noticeable in most of the developed countries in the northern hemisphere—in the OECD (Organization for Economic Co-operation and Development) countries, North America and North Asia.

Even though it is predicted that the world population will reach a plateau in 2050, in much of the developed world, it appears that the population is already plateauing.[286] With a sub-replacement fertility rate of less than 2.1 babies per woman, which is the critical number for population replacement,[287] population decline is what the future holds for most of the developed world. The issue of population decline is further exacerbated by the fact that many youth today, especially the millennials (people born between 1981 and

---

[285] 'The Future of Human Geography'[video], YouTube, posted by Parag Khanna, 17 June 2021, https://www.youtube.com/watch?v=FKexILzphoI, accessed August 2021.

[286] Ibid.

[287] James Gallagher, 'Remarkable Decline in Fertility Rates', *BBC*, 9 November 2018, available at: https://www.bbc.com/news/health-46118103. Accessed August 2021.

1996), are choosing not to have babies for economic, social and environmental reasons.[288]

An ageing population is a population that hinders productivity. Japan, the country with the oldest population in the world, also has the lowest productivity amongst the developed countries in the world.[289] The issue with the skewed ageing of the population of Japan is that there is no amount of capital investment that can reverse its productivity trend, especially when there is a lack of qualified youth workers.

In contrast, in most of the developing world, especially in most of South and Southeast Asia and the Pacific regions, there exist large numbers of young people.[290] The young people comprise three generational groups, the millennials, Generation Z (people born between 1997 and 2012) and Generation Alpha (people born or to be born in the period 2012 to 2025). Together, they constitute a demographic that is less than forty years of age. They represent the workforce of today and the future.

Given the youth influence, the future growth of a country or in this context, a modern organization, will be shaped by where they go and which companies they work for. Thus, the

---

[288] 'The Future of Human Geography'[video]. Interestingly, a study by Seth Wynes and Kimberley Nicholas showed that one less baby will help reduce greenhouse gas (GHG) emissions by 58.6 trillion tonnes (source: Seth Wynes and Kimberley Nicholas, 'The Four Lifestyle Choices that Most Reduce Your Carbon Footprint', Lund University, 12 July 2017, available at: https://www.lunduniversity.lu.se/article/four-lifestyle-choices-most-reduce-your-carbon-footprint. Accessed August 2021).

[289] 'Life in 2025: what will the future look like?', *Financial Times*, 16 December 2020, available at: https://www.ft.com/content/25ccd513-6b95-4596-a9d6-a74764fb3dc1. Accessed October 2021.

[290] 'The Future of Human Geography'[video], YouTube, posted by Parag Khanna, 17 June 2021, https://www.youtube.com/watch?v=FKexILzphoI. Accessed August 2021.

war for talent will intensify as companies in the developed countries pit against one another for youth workers. The war for youth talent is so critical that it should not be left only to the chief human resources officers to address. Rather, it should be addressed by the CEOs and boards of companies, as it will have a direct bearing on the company's overall strategy.

This begs the question: What must organizations do to attract the youth workers, especially millennials, who will represent 75 per cent of the working population, come 2025?[291]

To answer this question, let us turn to the research that has been conducted by Great Place to Work. According to its recent 2021 survey, there are five things that are important to millennials:[292]

1. *Fair pay and personal meaning:*

   At the top of the list of things that millennials want is fair pay and personal meaning or purpose. Millennials also prefer a work culture that fosters care and respect for one another at every level of the organization. If they perceive a misalignment between pay and meaning, the survey also showed that they will not hesitate to 'walk'. They are four times more likely to leave their jobs than Baby Boomers (people born between 1946 and 1964),

---

[291] CPA Australia, 'Organizations Must Exert Trust as Employees Increasingly Seek Remote Working Opportunities', *BBC Capital*, 2021, available at: http://www.bbc.com/storyworks/capital/the-rise-of-the-free-agent/embracing-the-mobile-workforce. Accessed August 2021.

[292] Claire Hastwell, 'Top 5 Things Millennials Want in the Workplace in 2021', Great Place to Work, 16 July 2021, available at: https://www.greatplacetowork.com/resources/blog/top-5-things-millennials-want-in-the-workplace-in-2021-as-told-by-millennials?utm_source=website_bw_millenials&utm_medium=promoted&utm_campaign=bw-millenials2021&utm_content=gptw_rhc. Accessed October 2021.

and eleven times more likely than Generation X (people between 1965 and 1980).

2. **Inclusive benefits:**

   Millennials look for companies that offer inclusive benefits. Benefits such as 'pawternity leave' are valued as many of them are choosing to have pets rather than children. It is for this reason why some companies have introduced pawternity benefits, of which HarperCollins Publishers is one example.[293]

3. **Gender equality:**

   It is another important factor for the millennials. There are now companies that actively work to elevate women to higher rungs of the organization, as well as put in place policies and practices to address the gender-based pay gap. As an example, the Zillow Group, an online real estate company, conducts salary reviews twice a year to ensure that there is pay parity between the genders at all the pay-grade levels.

4. **Flexible work arrangements:**

   Another strong desire that has been expressed by millennials is for flexible work arrangements. Given that work–life balance matters a lot to this generational group, they want to have the option to work flexibly and even remotely, either some of the time or all the time.

5. **A voice:**

   Millennials value a culture where they can be heard and have a sense of shared ownership and belonging. They thrive in a work culture that gives them psychological

---

[293] Somak Ghoshal, 'HarperCollins Publishers India Will Grant 'Pawternity Leave' To Employees Adopting Pets', *Huffington Post*, 6 April 2017, available at: https://www.huffpost.com/archive/in/entry/harpercollins-publishers-india-will-grant-pawternity-leave-to_a_22028162. Accessed October 2021.

safety to bring forward new ideas, push the envelope or have their voices heard when they disagree. Recognizing the importance of the millennial voice, DBS Bank provides a disproportionate share of voice to millennials to help develop new solutions and service offerings that appeal to the younger generation.[294]

To attract young talent, many leading companies, including Microsoft and SAP, have introduced early talent programmes 'to get them while they are young'.[295] Microsoft has a successful youth recruitment and accelerated development programme, called the 'Microsoft Academy of College Hires' (MACH). Every year, hundreds of MBA students from top business schools in the world apply to the prestigious programme. The MACH hires are put through a carefully curated year-long programme that is taught by top-notch professors from across the world. They are given lots of exposure to do impactful work and many opportunities to work in highly visible projects that give them direct access to Microsoft executives.

The SAP Next Talent programme[296] is another successful programme for attracting and retaining young talent, including millennials. It is an eighteen-month, full-time, rotational career accelerator programme that helps youth workers explore their interests and passions, while enabling them to do great work for SAP.

[294] Nik Gowing and Chris Langdon, Thinking the Unthinkable: A New Imperative for Leadership in the Digital Age (Suffolk: John Catt Educational Ltd), p. 163.

[295] Parag Khanna, *Move: The Forces Uprooting Us* (New York: Scribner, 2021), p. 40.

[296] 'SAP Next Talent', SAP, 2021, available at: https://www.sap.com/sea/about/careers/students-graduates/graduates/next-talent.html. Accessed October 2021.

Another interesting fact about millennials is that they prefer short-term assignments over long-term assignments (longer than a year in duration). They prefer to travel, rather than stay in one place, and favour experiences over rewards.[297] However, to our knowledge, we do not believe that there exist any such programmes that would allow millennials to off-ramp and on-ramp easily so they can pursue their other interests between jobs or tasks.

Geopolitics

Another disruptive force that is affecting the world of work is geopolitics. Geopolitics is one of the top concerns of business and corporate leaders.[298] It is also a factor that CEOs and business leaders have little control over.

Since the onset of the coronavirus pandemic, the global trend is moving towards protectionism, anti-foreign worker sentiment and national sovereignty. Many governments across the world have introduced policies to protect domestic jobs and local employment. Which is why immigration challenges are becoming a growing concern for companies, especially the multinational corporations which typically have a higher proportion of foreign talent, when compared to local companies.

---

[297] CPA Australia, `Organizations Must Exert Trust as Employees Increasingly Seek Remote Working Opportunities', BBC Capital, 2021, available at: http://www.bbc.com/storyworks/capital/the-rise-of-the-free-agent/embracing-the-mobile-workforce. Accessed August 2021.

[298] Alex Gray, 'This is What's Worrying CEOs the Most', World Economic Forum, 29 January 2016, available at: https://www.weforum.org/agenda/2016/01/this-is-what-s-worrying-ceos/. Accessed October 2021.

Companies now face tighter eligibility requirements for work authorizations and permits for their employees. The other challenges facing companies include more intense scrutiny and inspections at border crossings, and increased compliance enforcement. The intensification of these checks has a lot of downstream effects, including increased the risk of immigration and tax exposure for both the companies and the individuals.

Furthermore, other possible challenges include:[299]

- Thorough investigation and possible seizure of content and corporate data held on laptops and smartphone at border checks.
- Increased risk of entry being either refused or delayed.
- Increased risk of data sharing between immigration and the tax authorities.

As such, companies now face longer than normal processing times for work authorizations and permits, more onerous documentation submission, more frequent requests for evidence and a higher percentage of denials. And these changes in immigration policy have impacted services organizations the most, where specialist resources are flown into countries for short-term assignments or projects. One of our friends who works for General Electric, shared that it has been almost impossible to fly her services professionals and technology architects into most of the countries in Southeast Asia since the start of the pandemic.

---

[299] Naumaan Hameed, 'Geopolitical Impact on Global Immigration', KPMG, May 2019, available at: https://home.kpmg/xx/en/home/insights/2019/05/geopolitical-impact-on-global-immigration.html. Accessed September 2021.

Like many countries in the Asia-Pacific region, Singapore tightened its labour rules and raised the floor salary requirements for hiring foreign talents. From September 2020, the minimum salary requirement for an Employment Pass applicant was raised to S$4,500 (US$3,300) a month from the previous S$3,900 (US$2,800).[300] Higher floor thresholds have also been imposed for the financial sector and senior positions, to further protect jobs for Singapore citizens.[301]

The tightening of foreign labour market has repercussions for the modern organization. According to a recent survey by the American Chamber of Commerce,[302] more than half of the multinational companies surveyed conveyed that they faced difficulties in hiring locals with 'technical skills and knowledge'. 49 per cent of the companies also complained of a lack of creativity and critical thinking skills among locals. Figure 11.1 highlights the list of skills that are lacking in Singapore.

Technology

Technology is a major disruptive force that is impacting work in a significant way. Not only has technology helped organizations to improve productivity and efficiency in a big way by automating jobs, but it has also enabled organizations to adopt new business models, as well as new flexible work models for employees to work from home or remotely.

---

[300] Kentaro Iwamoto, 'Local Jobs or Global Talent? Singapore Faces COVID-era Conundrum', *Nikkei Asia*, 3 November 2020, available at: https://asia.nikkei.com/Spotlight/Asia-Insight/Local-jobs-or-global-talent-Singapore-faces-COVID-era-conundrum. Accessed September 2021.

[301] Ibid.

[302] Ibid.

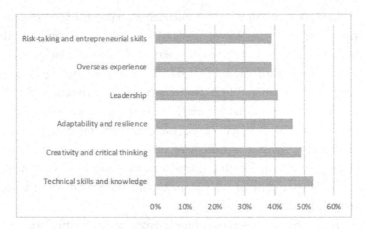

Figure 11.1: Skills That are Lacking in Singapore

Source: Adapted from Kentaro Iwamoto, 'Local Jobs or Global Talent?'.[303]

Given the ubiquitous influence of technology, digital competency is necessary for all employees and at all levels of the organization. Constant reskilling in digital competency is a must, due to the pace at which technology is advancing. The pace of technological advancement is so great that experts believe that there exists a skills gap that will continue to widen way into the future. The average shelf life of skills, which currently is at four years, is also expected to get shorter.[304]

---

[303] Adapted from Kentaro Iwamoto, 'Local Jobs or Global Talent? Singapore Faces COVID-era Conundrum', Nikkei Asia, 3 November 2020, available at: https://asia.nikkei.com/Spotlight/Asia-Insight/Local-jobs-or-global-talent-Singapore-faces-COVID-era-conundrum. Accessed September 2021.

[304] Wiley Education Services and Future Workplace, 'New Study Reveals Skills Gap Grew By Double Digits Since Last Year', *Business Wire*, 4 September 2019, available at: https://www.businesswire.com/news/home/20190904005094/en/New-Study-Reveals-Skills-Gap-Grew-By-Double-Digits-Since-Last-Year. Accessed September 2021.

Just as how disruptive innovations take root in simple applications at the lower end of a market, technological disruption also follows the same pattern by first displacing jobs at the lower end of the spectrum.[305] Thus, the low-level jobs are likely to be automated first. Robotic process automation (RPA) is a simple process that can replace the manual, administrative and tedious back-office tasks, such as copying and pasting information from a spreadsheet into a software application. In the past year, we saw many organizations adopting RPA, with almost 50 per cent of all companies in the world using it to streamline work.[306]

It is only a matter of time before all industries will be digitally overhauled. In the near future, it is estimated that more than 375 million people will have to switch occupations due to advancements in AI, robotics, 3D printing, IoT and automation.[307] By 2030, up to 800 million jobs and 20 per cent of today's global workforce will be replaced by robotic automation.[308]

---

[305] Karen Dillon, 'Disruption 2020: An Interview With Clayton M. Christensen', *MIT Sloan Management Review*, Spring 2020, available at: https://sloanreview.mit.edu/article/an-interview-with-clayton-m-christensen/. Accessed September 2021.

[306] UiPath, 'Study Finds Nearly 50% of Businesses Around the World Will Increase Robotic Process Automation Adoption due to COVID-19', *Business Wire*, 28 July 2020, available at: https://www.businesswire.com/news/home/20200728005136/en/Study-Finds-Nearly-50-of-Businesses-Around-the-World-Will-Increase-Robotic-Process-Automation-Adoption-due-to-COVID-19. Accessed October 2021.

[307] Khanna, *Move*, p. 31.

[308] James Manyika, Susan Lund, Michael Chui, Jacques Bughin, Jonathan Woetzel, Parul Batra, Ryan Ko and Saurabh Sanghvi, 'Jobs Lost, Jobs Gained: What the Future of Work will Mean for Jobs, Skills, and Wages', McKinsey Global Institute, 28 November 2017, available at: https://www.mckinsey.com/featured-insights/future-of-work/jobs-lost-jobs-gained-what-the-future-of-work-will-mean-for-jobs-skills-and-wages. Accessed October 2021.

The race against machines will be determined by the survival of the richest companies and the most technologically savvy and educated people. Coders, engineers and those with top-tier digital skills will stay ahead of robots and algorithms by being the ones designing them. In contrast, the low-level workers, who are also earn low wages, will continue to operate as cogs in the manufacturing, logistics, administrative industries, until their jobs become obsolete.

With data growing to the humongous amount of 175 zettabytes (10^{21}) and the world of work being connected to 50 billion interconnected devices,[309] it is foreseeable that these two trends, along with cloud computing, will define the technological landscape of the future. This is why Nadella said that we should think of work as one giant computer with all the elements of people, culture and data hanging off it:

> 'Digital technology, pervasively, is getting embedded in every place: every thing, every person, every walk of life is being fundamentally shaped by digital technology—it is happening in our homes, our work, our places of entertainment. It's amazing to think of a world as a computer. I think that's the right metaphor for us as we go forward . . . The idea that you can now use all of the computing power that is around you—this notion of the world as a computer—completely changes how you conduct a meeting and fundamentally what presence means for a meeting.'[310]

---

[309] Neha Alawadhi, 'Satya Nadella: A History Buff in School, says Sachin Yesterday, Virat Today', *Business Standard*, 27 February 2020, available at: https://www.business-standard.com/article/companies/satya-nadella-a-history-buff-in-school-says-sachin-yesterday-virat-today-120022600599_1.html. Accessed September 2021.

[310] Steve Ranger, 'Microsoft CEO Satya Nadella: The whole world is now a computer', *ZDnet*, 22 May 2018, available at: https://www.zdnet.

The use of AI also makes it possible to re-conceptualize work as a collaborative problem-solving effort, where humans define the problems, machines help find the solutions, and humans then verify the acceptability of those solutions. A healthcare initiative in the United Kingdom, where a group of specialists who are involved with a single patient, has been able to improve the quality of patient care with the use of AI and other digital tools. Not only has this technological solution been able to integrate their respective domain expertises, but has also been able to integrate the data from tests and medical monitors to alert if something unfortunate was about to happen to them.[311]

With technology at the centre of the Fourth Industrial Revolution, the lines between physical, digital and biological will become more blurred. Among the extended reality technologies that are available today, there is a growing trend for companies to adopt Augmented Reality (AR) to address workplace needs.[312] With AR, business professionals can access the information they need within seconds, without looking at a manual or seeking out assistance. The advancements in AR have also made it possible for humans and machines to collaborate to achieve results that neither could have done alone. For example, an engineer can wear a set of smart glasses to direct a virtual assistant to fix a technical problem on his or her smartphone.

---

com/article/microsoft-ceo-nadella-the-whole-world-is-now-a-computer/. Accessed October 2021.

[311] Peter Evans-Greenwood, Harvey Lewis and James Guszcza, 'Reconstructing Work: Automation, Artificial Intelligence and the Essential Role of Humans', *Deloitte Review*, Issue 21, July 2017, available at: https://www2.deloitte.com/content/dam/insights/us/articles/3883_Reconstructing-work/DUP_Reconstructing-work-reprint.pdf. Accessed October 2021.

[312] Rebekah Carter, 'The Role of AR in the Future of Work', *XR Today*, 30 April 2021, available at: https://www.xrtoday.com/augmented-reality/the-role-of-ar-in-the-future-of-work/. Accessed October 2021.

Another application of AR is in training. With an AR app and smart glasses, people can learn how to install a new software or how to troubleshoot a technical problem without stepping into a classroom.

Another trend that technology enables is digital mobility. We believe that digital mobility will be a major source of talent in the future. It enables organizations to reach talent outside their home countries and tap into the scarce youth resources, including millennials, who favour mobile and remote work. The biggest technological companies in the United States, including Microsoft and Cisco Systems, are already tapping into digital mobility to access and recruit talent through the use of cloud computing. When the United States' H1-B visa was suspended by the Trump administration, preventing Indian software engineers from going to the United States to work, many of the companies responded by outsourcing more work to Bangalore and Hyderabad,[313] thus being able to access talents outside of the United States for their purposes.

Upwork,[314] an AI-powered global job platform has been connecting companies with freelancers, independent talent and agencies from around the world, thus helping organizations to tap into a globally connected digital workforce.

Economic Impacts

During both the Global Financial Crisis and now the coronavirus pandemic, we saw how economic contraction has affected work, with millions of people being furloughed, laid off or asked to reduce their hours of work. In this past year, the pandemic which

---

[313] Parag Khanna, Move: The Forces Uprooting Us (New York: Scribner, 2021), p. 22.

[314] 'How It Works', Upwork, 2021, available at: https://www.upwork.com/i/how-it-works/client/. Accessed October 2021.

led to the Great Lockdown, affected 114 million job losses in 2020[315] around the world, of which there were 81 million jobs lost in the Asia-Pacific.[316] The number of working hours were also significantly reduced in 2020, amounting to an equivalent of 255 million full-time jobs or US$3.7 trillion in lost labour income.[317]

The economic contraction is affecting work by transforming the workforce. The trend is towards reducing traditional employment, resulting in a rise in the growth of alternative work arrangements and workers who are 'off the balance sheet'.[318] These contingent workers include gig workers, freelancers, temporary workers, part-time workers, contractors and other specialists, who are hired on a non-permanent basis and do not have full-time employment status.

It is expected that this group of workers will grow significantly, to as high as 40 per cent of workers in the near future.[319] Additionally, more than 80 per cent of large corporations

[315] Felix Richter, 'COVID-19 has Caused a Huge Amount of Lost Working Hours', World Economic Forum, 4 February 2021, available at: https://www.weforum.org/agenda/2021/02/covid-employment-global-job-loss/. Accessed July 2021.

[316] Sumit Agarwal, 'Commentary: The Gig Economy—a Surprise Boost from the Pandemic and in Singapore, it's not Going Anywhere', *Channel News Asia*, 9 March 2021, available at: https://www.channelnewsasia.com/news/commentary/gig-economy-performance-covid-19-jobs-revenue-grab-gojek-14288764. Accessed July 2021.

[317] Richter, 'COVID-19 has Caused a Huge Amount of Lost Working Hours'.

[318] Jeff Schwartz, Heather Stockton and Kelly Monahan, 'Forces of Change', The Future of Work Series, Deloitte Insights, July 2017, available at: https://www2.deloitte.com/content/dam/insights/us/articles/4322_Forces-of-change_FoW/DI_Forces-of-change_FoW.pdf. Accessed September 2021.

[319] Intuit, *Intuit 2020 Report*, October 2010, available at: http://http-download.intuit.com/http.intuit/CMO/intuit/futureofsmallbusiness/intuit_2020_report.pdf?_ga=1.82600086.1286327959.1409610840. Accessed October 2021.

plan to substantially increase their use of contingent workforce, making labour more of a variable cost, as they are unsure about how the economy will play out.

According to Deloitte,[320] there are four distinct segments of workers that exist in organizations today. The traditional full-time employee and the tenured remote worker are workers 'on the balance sheet'. Whereas the outside contractor and the transactional remote worker are workers who are off it. See

Table 11.1: Four Distinct Segments of Workers of the Future

On the Balance Sheet Workers	Off the Balance Sheet Workers
Traditional full-time employee • Costly to hire and retain • Aligned to the organizational culture	Outside contractor • Outsider mentality • Hired for project-based work • Typically, not assimilated to the organizational culture
Tenured remote worker • Isolated from headquarters • Lacks social connectivity	Transactional remote worker • Low quality touch points • Transactional relationship with the employer

Source: Adapted from Jeff Schwartz et al., 'Forces of Change'.

---

[320] Jeff Schwartz, Heather Stockton and Kelly Monahan, 'Forces of Change', The Future of Work Series, Deloitte Insights, July 2017, available at: https://www2.deloitte.com/content/dam/insights/us/articles/4322_Forces-of-change_FoW/DI_Forces-of-change_FoW.pdf. Accessed September 2021.

Table 11.1 for a brief description of the characteristics of each worker segment.

There are many benefits for organizations to use off-balance-sheet workers. The top two benefits include a more effective recruitment strategy, as well as the flexibility of hiring as and when needs arise. However, there are challenges involved in hiring these workers, of which, managing a high turnover of staff is one challenge. This can affect the relationships among the people left on the team.

Additionally, it could erode the organizational culture. The culture issue simply cannot be ignored, as having one consistent culture is critical for promoting shared values, as well as facilitating expected behaviours and clarifying the roles that each of the different workers play in contributing to organizational success.

Furthermore, in the world of work that exists today, there is a shift towards platform work. The likes of Upwork, Amazon, Uber and Airbnb are creating an employment form for 'organizations and individuals to exchange information, solve specific problems or provide specific services in exchange of payment.'[321]

The rise of platform work suggests that 'work is being disconnected from jobs, and jobs and work are being disconnected from companies.'[322] One interesting aspect of platform work is that it gives organizations the advantage to 'tap into the brains

---

[321] European Observatory of Working Life, 'Platform Work', Eurofound, 29 June 2018, available at: https://www.eurofound.europa.eu/observatories/eurwork/industrial-relations-dictionary/platform-work. Accessed October 2021.

[322] Cathy Engelbert and John Hagel, 'Radically Open: Tom Friedman on Jobs, Learning and the Future of Work', Deloitte Insights, July 2017, available at: https://www2.deloitte.com/content/dam/insights/us/articles/3932_Radically-open/DUP_Radically-open-reprint.pdf. Accessed October 2021.

of anybody',[323] as well as access the critical skills of a global pool of workers. Through platforms, organizations can connect with independent professionals instantly, assign them tasks and have them start almost immediately. Like the challenges of managing a multi-segmented group of workers, instilling a common culture would be key for integrating these platform workers with the rest of the organization.

Managerial Implications

Managerial implications arising from these four disruptive forces on future work are:

- The war for talent will continue to intensify, especially for youth workers in the developed countries—a scarce resource. This war of talent will be felt and seen within and across sectors.
    - ° Hence, organizations will need to adopt a strategy that enables them 'get them while they are young' in order to attract and retain millennials.
    - ° Another important strategy is to adopt a digital mobility strategy like what the Silicon Valley companies have done—accessing the youth resources where they are based or where they want to be based.
- With millennials representing 75 per cent of the workforce in the not-so-distant future, organizations will have to be creative to introduce 'off-ramp' and 'on-ramp' work policies to give millennials the flexibility to travel while they are at the peaks of their working

---

[323] Ibid.

careers. Perhaps organizations might want to borrow a leaf from leading universities like INSEAD, that offer their students the opportunity to study from any of their four campuses in Asia, Europe, Middle East and the United States.

- There is no denying that geopolitical disruptions will hinder organizations from hiring foreign talents. This is yet another reason why organizations need to be proactive about their future capability plans, while in the meantime, leveraging technology as much as possible, to get work done while overcoming immigration challenges.

- As technology becomes more integrated with human beings, it is recommended that organizations look at ways to integrate work between humans and machines using AI, data and cloud computing. This will be an interesting challenge—to design work that involves human–machine, machine–human, human–human and machine–machine interactions.

- Organizations also need to build and foster a culture that will help them manage a diverse workforce, in which some workers will be on the balance sheets, while others will be off it, including platform workers. This means that organizations need to be adaptive and agile so that new organizational structures and teams can be formed easily when faced with challenges due to any of the disruptive forces.

- And finally, the greatest danger in times of turbulence is not the turbulence itself, but to act with today's logic especially while managing the three elements of a successful organization—people, culture and data.

Afterword

- What will the world of work look like?
- What does it take to stay ahead of the curve?
- How can individuals and organizations future proof themselves in this era of rapid change?

These questions have been at the top of our minds and were the motivational drivers for us to write this book about people, culture and data.

Hopefully our ideas, stories and case studies have produced something useful to help you manage the modern organization.

Please do share with us what you have learned from your leadership journey and we will continue to do the same. You are encouraged to connect with us on LinkedIn at: https://sg.linkedin.com/in/jaclynleephd (Jaclyn Lee) and https://sg.linkedin.com/in/jovinaang (Jovina Ang).

Acknowledgements

There are many people who have been important in our lives and careers.

Our families and the support system of our friends, without whom we would not be where we are, nor have the knowledge to write this book.

Our bosses, mentors, allies and supporters—past and present, who have constantly stretched and transformed us to become better leaders and human beings.

And you—for reading this book. We hope this book would be useful for you to manage and navigate effectively the complexities that confront us all in this new world of work.

Bibliography

Chapter 1

Barber, Felix, and Rainer Strack. 'The Surprising Economics of a "People Business"'. *Harvard Business Review*, 83 (6) (2005), pp. 80–90.

Cameron, Kim S., and Robert E. Quinn. *Diagnosing and Changing Organizational Culture: Based on the Competing Values Framework.* Third Edition. San Francisco, CA: Jossey-Bass, 2011.

Chatman, Jenny, and Francesca Gino. 'Don't Let the Pandemic Sink Your Company Culture'. *Harvard Business Review*, 17 August 2020. Available at: https://hbr.org/2020/08/dont-let-the-pandemicsink-your-company-culture [(Accessed September 2021).

Clarke, Alyson. 'Prioritise Culture Change to Accelerate Digital Transformation'. *Forrester*, 2018. Available at: https://go.forrester.com/blogs/prioritize-culture-change-to-acceleratedigital-transformation/ (Accessed September 2021).

Deady, Cormac, Conor McCarthy and Sinad Egan. 'Conscious Culture Creation: Seizing New Ways of Working'. KPMG. Available at: https://assets.kpmg/content/dam/kpmg/ie/pdf/2020/11/ie-conscious-culture-creation-seizing-new-waysof-working.pdf (Accessed September 2021).

De Smet, Aaron, Bonnie Dowling, Marino Mugayar-Baldocchi, and Bill Schaninger. 'Great Attrition or Great Attraction, the Choice is Yours'. McKinsey, 8 September 2021. Available at: https://www.mckinsey.com/business-functions/organization/our-insights/great-attrition-or-great-attraction-the-choice-isyours?cid=other-soc-lkn-mip-mck-oth-2109--&sid=5488984174&linkId=131747759 (Accessed September 2021).

'2021 Global Human Capital Trends: Special Report', December 2020. Deloitte. Available at: https://www2.deloitte.com/us/en/insights/focus/human-capital-trends.html (Accessed September 2021).

Emmett, Jonathan, Gunnar Schrah, Matt Schrimper, and Alexandra Wood. 'COVID-19 and the Employee Experience: How Leaders Can Seize the Moment'. McKinsey, 29 June 2020. Available at: https://www.mckinsey.com/business-functions/organization/our-insights/covid-19-and-the-employee-experience-howleaders-can-seize-the-moment# (Accessed September 2021).

Fralinger, Barbara, and Valerie Olson. 'Organizational Culture at the University Level: A Study Using the OCAI Instrument'. *Journal of College Teaching & Learning* (TLC) 4, (11) (2007). Available at: https://doi.org/10.19030/tlc.v4i11.1528 (Accessed October 2021).

Franklin, Daniel. *Mega Tech: Technology in 2050*. London: Profile Books, 2017.

Goran, Julie, Laura LaBerge and Ramesh Srinivasan. 'Culture for a Digital Age'. *McKinsey Quarterly* 3, 2017, pp. 56–67. Available at: https://www.mckinsey.com/businessfunctions/mckinsey-digital/our-insights/culture-for-a-digitalage (Accessed September 2021).

Gurehiek, Kathy. 'Research: Employees Rely on Employer Culture to Navigate Pandemic'. *SHRM HR Magazine*, 9 September 2021. Available at: https://www.shrm.org/hr-today/news/hr-news/pages/research-employees-rely-on-employerculture-to-navigate-pandemic.aspx (Accessed September 2021).

Harbert, Tam. 'The Pandemic Has Expanded the Role of HR'. *SHRM HR Magazine*, Fall, 1 September 2021. Available at: https://www.shrm.org/hr-today/news/hr-magazine/fall2021/Pages/pandemic-expands-role-of-hr.aspx (Accessed September 2021).

'How Air Asia Founder Tony Fernandes' Dream Came True'. *BBC*, 1 November 2010. Available at: https://www.bbc.com/news/business-11647205 (Accessed September 2021).

Khurana, Anil, Roger Wery and Amy Peirce. 'Using Data to Fuel Your Business Resilience in the Post-COVID-19 World'. PwC, 2 February 2021. Available at: https://www.pwc.com.au/digitalpulse/data-transformation-insights-coronavirus.html (Accessed September 2021).

Lee, Jaclyn. *Accelerating Organization Culture Change: Innovation Through Digital Tools*. Emerald Group Publishing, 2020.

Maslow, Abraham. 'Maslow's Hierarchy of Needs'. Index of DOCS/Teacing (sp), Collection/Honolulu, 1943.

Maylett, Tracy, and Matthew Wride. *The Employee Experience: How to Attract Talent, Retain Top Performers, and Drive Results*. New Jersey: John Wiley & Sons, 2017.

National Broadcast. 'PM Lee Hsien Loong: Overcoming the Crisis of a Generation'. Gov.sg, 7 June 2020. Available at: https://www.gov.sg/article/pm-lee-hsien-loong-overcomingthe-crisis-of-a-generation (Accessed September 2021).

Park, Namgyoo K. 'The Cultural Impact of Automation: Quality of Work and Life Redefined'. *Transformation of Work in Asia Pacific in the 21 Century* (HKUST Business School and APRU, 2018), pp. 129–164.

Van den Berg, Peter T., and Celeste PM Wilderom. 'Defining, Measuring and Comparing Organizational Cultures'. *Applied Psychology*, 53 (4) (2004), pp. 570–582.

Waller, David. '10 steps to Creating a Data-driven Culture'. *Harvard Business Review*, 6 February 2020. Available at: https://hbr.org/2020/02/10-steps-to-creating-a-data-drivenculture2-7 (Accessed September 2021).

West, Mike. *People Analytics for Dummies*, Tantor Media, 2020.

Chapter 2

Ardern, Jacinda. 'Conversations Through COVID-19: Rachel Taulelei'. COVID-19 Podcast Series, Facebook, 25 April 2020. Available at: https://www.facebook.com/

jacindaardern/videos/conversations-through-covid-19-racheltaulelei/588816781992136/ (Accessed July 2021).

'Atlassian Team Playbook: Building Strong Teams with Plays'. Atlassian, 2021. Available at: https://www.atlassian.com/team-playbook (Accessed September 2021).

Baker, Mary. '9 Future of Work Trends Post-COVID-19'. *Gartner*, 8 June 2020. Available at: https://www.gartner.com/smarterwithgartner/9-future-of-work-trends-post-covid-19/. (Accessed July 2021).

Bersin, Josh. 'Remote Work Has Arrived, But It's Not Quite As Great As We Hoped'. Joshbersin.com, 10 January 2021. Available at: https://joshbersin.com/2021/01/remote-work-has-arrivedbut-its-not-as-great-as-we-hoped/ (Accessed July 2021).

Co, Cindy. 'Work-from-Home to Remain as Default; Jobs Support Scheme Extended to July 9'. *Channel News Asia*, 18 June 2021. Available at: https://www.channelnewsasia.com/news/singapore/work-from-home-wfh-default-jobs-supportscheme-covid-19-15040560 (Accessed July 2021).

'Competing in 2020: Winners and Losers in the Digital Economy'. *Harvard Business Review*, 25 April 2017. Available at: https://hbr.org/sponsored/2017/04/competing-in-2020-winners-andlosers-in-the-digital-economy (Accessed July 2021).

Curran, Enda. 'Work From Home to Lift Productivity by 5% in Post-Pandemic U.S.'. *Bloomberg*, 22 April 2021. Available at: https://www.bloomberg.com/news/articles/2021-04-22/yesworking-from-home-makes-you-more-productive-study-finds (Accessed July 2021).

Doherty, Sharon. 'Building An Inclusive And Remote Culture'. *Forbes*, 3 August 2020. Available at: https://www.forbes.com/sites/forbeshumanresourcescouncil/2020/08/03/building-aninclusive-and-remote-culture/?sh=6d7a8bad279b (Accessed September 2021).

Gilchrist, Karen. 'The Pandemic has Boosted Freelance Work—and Hiring for These Jobs is Booming'. *CNBC Make It*, 6 July 2020. Available at: https://www.cnbc.com/2020/07/07/freelance-work-grows-amid-covid-19-math-stats-game-hiringin-demand.html (Accessed July 2021).

Hern, Alex. 'Microsoft Productivity Score Feature Criticised as Workplace Surveillance'. *The Guardian*, 24 November 2020. Available at: https://www.theguardian.com/technology/2020/nov/26/microsoft-productivity-score-feature-criticisedworkplace-surveillance (Accessed July 2021).

'How the Pandemic Changed Talent Management for the Better', Episode 817, *HBR Ideacast with Johnny C. Taylor Jr.* [podcast]. *Harvard Business Review*, 31 August 2021. Available at: https://hbr.org/podcast/2021/08/how-the-pandemic-changed-talentmanagement (Accessed September 2021).

Katella, Kathy. '5 Things to Know About the Delta Variant'. *Yale Medicine*, 6 January 2022. Available at: https://www.yalemedicine.org/news/5-things-to-know-delta-variant-covid (Accessed February 2022).

Kazi, Chandni, and Claire Hastwell. 'Remote Work Productivity Study Finds Surprising Reality: 2-Year Analysis'. Great Place to Work, 10 February 2021. Available at: https://

www.greatplacetowork.com/resources/blog/remote-workproductivity-study-finds-surprising-reality-2-year-study (Accessed July 2021).

Kit, Tang See. 'Goodbye Office: Is the Future of Work in Our Homes? *Channel News Asia*, 25 May 2020. Available at: https://www.channelnewsasia.com/news/business/goodbye-officework-from-home-future-covid-19-12758558 (Accessed August 2021).

Kropp, Brian. 'The Future of Employee Monitoring'. *Gartner*, 3 May 2019. Available at: https://www.gartner.com/smarterwithgartner/the-future-of-employee-monitoring/ (Accessed July 2021).

Lee, Jung Woo, and M. Jae Moon. 'Coming Age of Digital Automation: Backgrounds and Prospects'. *Transformation of Work in Asia Pacific in the 21 Century*. Association of Pacific Rim Universities, 2018. pp. 11–56.

Mann, Sandi, and Lynn Holdsworth. 'The Psychological Impact of Teleworking: Stress, Emotions and Health'. *New Technology, Work and Employment*, 2 October 2003. Available at: https://doi.org/10.1111/1468-005X.00121 (Accessed September 2021).

'MetLife's 18 Annual US Employee Benefit Trends Study 2020'. MetLife, 2021. Available at: https://www.metlife.com/employee-benefit-trends/ebts2020-holistic-well-being-drivesworkforce-success/ (Accessed July 2021).

'Report: Remote Work in the Age of COVID-19'. Slack, 21 April 2020. Available at: https://slack.com/intl/en-sg/

blog/collaboration/report-remote-work-during-coronavirus (Accessed September 2021).

'Omicron Variant: What You Need to Know', Centres for Disease Control and Prevention. 2 February 2022. Available at: https://www.cdc.gov/coronavirus/2019-ncov/variants/omicron-variant.html (Accessed February 2022).

Pande, Girija, and Frederic Donck. 'Digitalisation is Growing, so is its Carbon Footprint'. *Straits Times*, 13 August 2021. Available at: https://www.straitstimes.com/opinion/digitalisation-isgrowing-so-is-its-carbon-footprint (Accessed September 2021).

Parker, Kim, Juliana Menasce Horowitz, and Rachel Minkin, 'How the Coronavirus Outbreak Has—and Hasn't—Changed the Way Americans Work'. Pew Research Centre, 9 December 2020. Available at: https://www.pewresearch.org/socialtrends/2020/12/09/how-the-coronavirus-outbreak-has-andhasnt-changed-the-way-americans-work/ (Accessed July 2021).

Schawbel, Dan. 'The Balancing Act: What We've Learned from One Year of Working from Home'. World Economic Forum, 23 April 2021. Available at: https://www.weforum.org/agenda/2021/04/working-from-home-what-we-learned/ (Accessed July 2021).

Seabrook, John. 'Has the Pandemic Transformed the Office Forever?'. *The New Yorker*, 25 January 2021. Available at: https://www.newyorker.com/magazine/2021/02/01/has-thepandemic-transformed-the-office-forever (Accessed September2021).

Spotify Training & Development, 'Spotify Engineering Culture—Part 1' [video], 3:05 to 4:12, 2013. Available at: https://vimeo.com/85490944 (Accessed September 2021).

Teevan, Jaime, Brent Hecht, and Sonia Jaffe. 'The New Future of Work: Research from Microsoft on the Impact of the Pandemic on Work Practices' (First edn.). Microsoft, 2021. Available at: https://aka.ms/newfutureofwork.Microsoft (Accessed July 2021).

Thomason, Bobbi. 'Help Your Team Beat WFH Burnout'. *Harvard Business Review*, 26 January 2021. Available at: https://hbr.org/2021/01/help-your-team-beat-wfh-burnout (Accessed July 2021).

Ulpah, Maryah, Hanifa Maher Denny, and Siswi Jayanti. 'Studi Tentang Faktor Individu, Lingkungan Kerja Komputer dan Keluhan Computer Vision Syndrome (CVS) pada Pengguna Komputer di Perusahaan Perakitan Mobil'. *Jurnal Kesehatan Masyarakat*, 3 (3) (2017), pp. 513–523.

Wang, Yeli, Monica Palanichamy Kala, and Tazeen H. Jafar. 'Factors Associated with Psychological Distress During the Coronavirus Disease 2019 (COVID-19) Pandemic on the Predominantly General Population: A Systematic Review and Meta-analysis' *PLOS ONE*, December 2020, available at: https://doi.org/10.1371/journal.pone.0244630 (Accessed September 2021).

Walters, Cara. 'Four Times a Year in the Office: Atlassian Goes All in on WFH'. *The Sydney Morning Herald*, 29 April 2021. Available at: https://www.smh.com.au/business/smallbusiness/four-times-a-year-in-the-office-atlassian-goes-all-inon-wfh-20210428-p57n4w.html (Accessed July 2021).

Westcott, Ben. 'Delta Variant Outbreak Threatens Singapore's Living with COVID model'. *CNN*, 7 September 2021. Available at: https://edition.cnn.com/2021/09/07/asia/singapore-covid-19-restrictions-intl-hnk/index.html (Accessed September 2021).

Wiles, Jackie. '9 Questions That Should Be in Every Employee Engagement Survey'. *Gartner*, 22 August 2020. Available at: https://www.gartner.com/smarterwithgartner/the-9-questionsthat-should-be-in-every-employee-engagement-survey/ (Accessed July 2021).

Chapter 3

Bass, Bernard M., and Ronald E. Riggio. *Transformational Leadership*. New Jersey: Lawrence Erlbaum Associates, Inc., 2006.

Borman, Walter C., and Donald H. Brush. 'More Progress Toward a Taxonomy of Managerial Performance Requirements', *Human Performance 6*, no. 1 (1993), pp. 1–21.

Burns, James MacGregor. *Leadership*. New York: Harper and Row, 1978. pp. 141–400.

Cohan, Peter. 'Culture Is The Most Surprising Reason Microsoft Stock Will Keep Rising'. *Forbes*, 30 January 2020. Available at: https://www.forbes.com/sites/petercohan/2020/01/30/culture-is-the-most-surprising-reason-microsoft-stock-willkeep-rising/?sh=159daca41b23 (Accessed September 2021).

Corporate Longevity Forecast'. *Innosight*, May 2021. Available at: https://www.innosight.com/insight/creative-destruction/ (Accessed August 2021).

Dweck, Carol, and Kathleen Hogan. 'How Microsoft Uses a Growth Mindset to Develop Leaders'. *Harvard Business Review*, 7 October 2016. Available at: https://hbr.org/2016/10/how-microsoft-uses-a-growth-mindset-to-develop-leaders (Accessed September 2021).

Dweck, Carol S. *Mindset: The New Psychology of Success*. New York: Random House, 2008.

Estrin, James. 'Kodak's First Digital Moment'. *The New York Times*, 12 August 2015. Available at: https://lens.blogs.nytimes.com/2015/08/12/kodaks-first-digital-moment/ (Accessed September 2021).

Favaro, Ken. 'Strategy or Culture: Which Is More Important?' *Strategy-Business*, 22 May 2014. Available at: https://www.strategy-business.com/blog/Strategy-or-Culture-Which-Is-More-Important (Accessed September 2021).

Harvard Business Review, March–April 1990. Available at: https://hbr.org/1990/03/the-managers-job-folklore-and-fact (Accessed September 2021).

Hempel, Jessi. 'Microsoft in the Age of Satya Nadella'. *Wired*, February 2015. Available at: https://www.wired.com/2015/01/microsoft-nadella/ (Accessed September 2021).

Johnson, Jamie. '10 Bill Gates Quotes Every Business Owner Needs to Hear'. *CO* by U.S. Chamber of Commerce, 10 January 2020. Available at: https://www.uschamber.com/co/start/strategy/bill-gates-business-quotes (Accessed September 2021).

Judge, Timothy A., and Ronald F. Piccolo. 'Transformational and Transactional Leadership: A Meta-Analytic Test of Their Relative Validity'. *Journal of Applied Psychology*, 89, no. 5, 2004, pp. 755–768.

Koulopoulos, Thomas. '5 Unforgettable Leadership Lessons From "Manager of the Century" Jack Welch'. *Inc*, 2 March 2020. Available at: https://www.inc.com/thomas-koulopoulos/jackwelch-ceo-general-electric-business-leadership-managementlessons.html (Accessed September 2021).

'Learning to Be a Better Leader', Knowledge@Wharton, 20 July 2021. Available at: https://knowledge.wharton.upenn.edu/article/learning-to-be-a-better-leader/ (Accessed September 2021).

'Market Capitalisation of Microsoft (MSFT)', 2021. Companies Market Capitalisation. Available at: https://companiesmarketcap.com/microsoft/marketcap/ (Accessed September 2021).

Microsoft 365 Team, 'Grow Your Business with a Growth Mindset', *Microsoft*, 12 June 2020. Available at: https://www.microsoft.com/en-us/microsoft-365/business-insightsideas/resources/grow-your-business-with-a-growth-mindset (Accessed September 2021).

Useem, Michael. *The Edge: How Ten CEOs Learned to Lead—And the Lessons for Us All*. London: Hachette, 2021.

Mintzberg, Henry. 'The Manager's Job: Forklore and Fact'.

Nadella, Satya, Greg Shaw, and Jill Tracie Nichols. *Hit Refresh: The Quest to Rediscover Microsoft's Soul and Imagine a Better Future for Everyone.* London: HarperCollins, 2017. p.101.

Nichols, Chris. 'Fact-check: Have One-third of US Small Businesses Closed during Pandemic?'. *Austin American-Statesman*, 8 June 2021. Available at: https://www.statesman. com/story/news/politics/politifact/2021/06/08/kamala-harris-smallbusiness-closures-covid-fact-check/7602531002/ (Accessed September 2021).

Perry, Mark J. 'Fortune 500 Firms in 1955 vs. 2014; 88% are Gone, and We're All Better off Because of that Dynamic "Creative Destruction"'. *AEIdeas*, 18 August 2014. Available at: https://www.aei.org/carpe-diem/fortune-500-firms-in-1955-vs-2014-89-are-gone-and-were-all-better-off-because-of-thatdynamic-creative-destruction/ (Accessed September 2021).

Tett, Gillian. *Anthro-Vision: A New Way to See in Business and Life,* New York: Simon and Schuster, 2021.

'The Big Read: COVID-19 Decimated Their Promising Business, but Some Entrepreneurs aren't Afraid to Try Again'. *Channel News Asia*, 26 April 2021. Available at: https:// www.channelnewsasia.com/singapore/big-read-covid-19-decimatedtheir-promising-business-some-entrepreneurs-arent-afraid-tryagain-241866 (Accessed September 2021).

Useem, Michael. *The Edge: How Ten CEOs Learned to Lead—And the Lessons for Us All.* London: Hachette, 2021.

Viguerie, Patrick S., Ned Calder, and Brian Hindo. '2021 Corporate Longevity Forecast'. *Innosight*, May 2021. Available at: https://www.innosight.com/insight/creative-destruction/ (Accessed August 2021).

Vozza, Stephanie. 'Six Habits Of People Who Know How To Bring Out The Best In Others'. *Fast Company*, 1 May 2016. Available at: https://www.fastcompany.com/3054826/ sixhabits-of-people-who-know-how-to-bring-out-the-best-inothersm (Accessed September 2021).

Welch, Jack, Suzy Welch, Bodo Primus, Helmut Winkelmann, Susanne Grawe, and Marian Szymczyk. *Winning*. New York: HarperCollins, 2005.

Ward, Patrick. 'Management Theory of Henri Fayol: Summary, Examples'. *NanoGlobals*, 29 August 2021. Available at: https:// nanoglobals.com/glossary/henri-fayol-management-theory/ (Accessed September 2021).

Chapter 4

Bhageshpur, Kiran. 'Data is the New Oil and That's a Good Thing'. *Forbes*, 15 November 2019. Available at: https:// www.forbes.com/sites/forbestechcouncil/2019/11/15/data-is-thenew-oil-and-thats-a-good-thing/?sh=3d22a6d17304 (Accessed October 2021).

Cukier, Kenneth. 'The data-driven world'. *Mega Tech: Technology in 2050*.

Díaz, Alejandro, Kayvaun Rowshankish, and Tamim Saleh. 'Why data culture matters'. *McKinsey Quarterly*, No. 3, 2018.

Available at: https://www.mckinsey.com/~/media/mckinsey/
business%20functions/mckinsey%20analytics/our%20
insights/mckinsey%20quarterly%202018%20number%20
3%20overview%20and%20full%20issue/mckinsey-quarterly-
2018-number-3.ashx (Accessed September 2021).

Diez, Fermin, Mark Bussin and Venessa Lee. *Fundamentals of HR
Analytics: A Manual on Becoming HR Analytical.* Bingley: Emerald
Group Publishing, 2019.

Ericsson Mobility Report 2021, June 2021. Ericsson. Available at:
https://www.ericsson.com/4a03c2/assets/local/mobilityreport/
documents/2021/june-2021-ericsson-mobility-report.pdf
(Accessed October 2021).

Frankiewicz, Becky, and Tomas Chamorro-Premuzic. 'The Post-
Pandemic-Rules of Talent Management'. *Harvard Business Review*,
13 October 2020. Available at: https://hbr.org/2020/10/
the-post-pandemic-rules-of-talent-management   (Accessed
September 2021).

Franklin, Daniel. 'Introduction' in *Mega Tech: Technology in
2050.* Ericsson, *Ericsson Mobility Report 2021*, June 2021.
Available at: https://www.ericsson.com/4a03c2/assets/local/
mobilityreport/documents/2021/june-2021-ericsson-mobility-
report.pdf (Accessed October 2021).

Grace, Emily. 'How Google is using people analytics to completely
reinvent HR'. *PeopleHum*, 10 August 2020. Available at: https://
www.peoplehum.com/blog/how-googleis-using-people-
analytics-to-completely-reinvent-hr (Accessed September 2021).

Ismail, Nick. 'From Just Visible to Truly Valuable: How to Manage Big Data in the Age of Digital'. *Information Age*, 13 January 2017. Available at: https://www.information-age. com/how-manage-bigdata-digital-age-123463978/ (Accessed October 2021).

Janager, Ritu. 'Data is the New Oil'. *The Commerce Society*, 10 June 2021. Available at: https://comsocsrcc.com/data-is-thenew-oil/ (Accessed September 2021).

Kotorchevikj, Ivana. 'The Role of People Analytics in Managing the COVID-19 Crisis in the Organization'. *Towards Data Science*, 31 August 2020. Available at: https://towardsdatascience.com/ the-role-of-people-analytics-in-managing-the-covid-19-crisisin-the-organization-8d25070569b (Accessed October 2021).

Ledet, Elizabeth, Keith McNulty, Daniel Morales, and Marissa Shandell. 'How to be Great at People Analytics'. McKinsey, 2 October 2020. Available at: https://www.mckinsey.com/ business-functions/organization/our-insights/how-to-begreat-at-people-analytics (Accessed September 2021).

Mlitz, Kimberly. 'Big Data and Business Analytics Revenue Worldwide 2015–2022'. *Statista*. Available at: https:// www.statista.com/statistics/551501/worldwide-big-data-businessanalytics-revenue/ (Accessed October 2021).

Reiner, Juergen. 'Preparing for Digital as the New Normal'. *Oliver Wyman*, November 2017, p.2. Available at: https:// www.oliverwyman.com/content/dam/oliver-wyman/ v2/publications/2017/nov/Preparing-for-digital-as-the-newnormal.pdf (Accessed September 2021).

Chapter 5

Atkins, Charles, Mitra Mahdavian, Katelyn McCarthy, and Michael Viertier. 'Starting the Analytics Journey: Where You Can Find Sales Growth Right Now'. McKinsey, 18 April 2018. Available at: https://www.mckinsey.com/business-functions/marketing-and-sales/our-insights/starting-the-analyticsjourney (Accessed September 2021).

Carande, Carl, Paul Lipinski, and Traci Gusher. 'How to Integrate Data and Analytics into Every Part of Your Organization'. *Harvard Business Review*, 23 June 2017. Available at: https://hbr.org/2017/06/how-to-integrate-data-and-analytics-into-everypart-of-your-organization (Accessed September 2021).

Cameron, Kim and Robert Quinn. 'About the Organizational Culture Assessment Instrument (OCAI)', n.d.m. Available at: https://www.ocai-online.com/about-the-Organizational-Culture-Assessment-Instrument-OCAI (Accessed October 2021).

Griffin, Jane, and Tom Davenport. 'Organising Analytics from the Inside Out'. Deloitte, 2014. Available at: https://www2.deloitte.com/content/dam/Deloitte/us/Documents/deloitteanalytics/us-da-organizing-analytics-inside-out.pdf (Accessed October 2021).

Goasduff, Laurrence. 'Avoid 5 Pitfalls When Building Data and Analytics Teams'. *Gartner*, 9 July 2020. Available at: https://www.gartner.com/smarterwithgartner/avoid-5-pitfalls-whenbuilding-data-and-analytics-teams (Accessed October 2021).

Kaplan, Robert S., and David Norton. 'The Balanced Scorecard: Measures that Drive Performance'. *Harvard Business Review*, 70 (1), January–February 1992, pp. 71–79.

Kaplan, Robert S., and David P. Norton. *The Balanced Scorecard— Translating Strategy into Action*. Boston: Harvard Business School Press, 1996.

Miranda, Gloria Macías-Lizaso. 'Building an Effective Analytics Organization'. McKinsey, 18 October 2018. Available at: https://www.mckinsey.com/industries/financial-services/ourinsights/building-an-effective-analytics-organization (Accessed September 2021.)

Parikh, Milind. 'Critical Success Factors to Setting up a Data and Analytics Organization'. LinkedIn Pulse, 9 January 2018. Available at: https://www.linkedin.com/pulse/critical-successfactors-setting-up-data-analytics-parikh-cisa-pmp/ (Accessed September 2021).

'Project Marvel' [video], YouTube, posted by DBS, 21 February 2017. Available at: https://www.youtube.com/watch?v=IjOH4eHSlSY (Accessed October 2021).

SAP, *Integrated Reports 2019 on Work Performance*. Available at: https://www.sap.com/integrated-reports/2019/en/socialperformance.html (Accessed October 2021).

'The Kirkpatrick Model'. Kirkpatrick Partners. Available at: https://www.kirkpatrickpartners.com/Our-Philosophy/The-Kirkpatrick-Model. (Accessed October 2021)

Vulpen, Erik Van. 'The HR Scorecard: A Full Guide', AIHR. Available at: https://www.aihr.com/blog/hr-scorecard/ (Accessed October 2021)

Chapter 6

Cao, Heng, Jianying Hu, Chen Jiang, Tarun Kumar, Ta-Hsin Li, Yang Liu, Yingdong Lu, Shilpa Mahatma, Aleksandra Mojsilović, Mayank Sharma, Mark S. Squillante, and Yichong Yu. 'OnTheMark: Integrated Stochastic Resource Planning of Human Capital Supply Chains'. *INFORMS Journal on Applied Analytics*, 41(5), 2011, pp.414–435. Available at: https://doi.org/10.1287/inte.1110.0596 (Accessed October 2021).

Größler, Andreas, and Alexander Zock. 'Supporting Long-Term Workforce Planning with a Dynamic Aging Chain Model—A Case Study from the Service Industry'. *Human Resource Management*, 49 (5), September–October 2010, pp.829–848.

Kamph, Brad. 'Put the Dynamics of the Workforce Supply Chain to Work for You'. *Power Magazine*, 15 January 2007. Available at: https://www.powermag.com/put-the-dynamicsof-the-workforce-supply-chain-to-work-for-you/ (Accessed October 2021).

Miller, Stephen. 'Applying Analytics can Enhance Workforce Planning'. *Strategic HR Management*, 19 June 2016. Available at: https://www.shrm.org/hr-today/news/hr-news/pages/workforce- analytics.aspx (Accessed September 2021).

Mutsuddi, Indranil. 'Supply Chain Management Effective People Management'. *Journal of Operations Management*, 11 (4), November 2012, pp. 53–64.

Chapter 7

Bersin, Josh. 'Big Data in Human Resources: A World of Haves And Have-Nots'. *Forbes*, 7 October 2013. Available at: https://www.forbes.com/sites/joshbersin/2013/10/07/big-data-in-human resources a world of haves and havenots/?sh=cad265a200fd (Accessed June 2021).

Excerpt from 'OCBC's Head of Group HR, Jason Ho on "Adaptable HR"', LaptrinhX, 20 July 2020. Available at: https://laptrinhx.com/ocbc-s-head-of-group-hr-jason-ho-onadaptable-hr-2563107920/ (Accessed June 2021).

'Group Business Overview', 2021. OCBC Bank. Available at: https://www.ocbc.com/group/about-us/group-business(Accessed June 2021).

Hernandez, Nelissa. 'Jason Ho: A Digital Strategy is Also About People', Infocomm Media Development Authority, 22 May 2019. Available at: https://www.imda.gov.sg/news-and-events/impact-news/2018/02/jason-ho-a-digital-strategy-is-alsoabout-people (Accessed June 2021).

Human Capital Partnership Quarterly e-Bulletin, Number 16, April 2021. Tripartite Alliance. Available at: https://www.tal.sg/tafep/-/media/TAL/Tafep/Resources/Publications/Files/2021/HCP-Ebulletin-Issue-16_April-June-2021)pdf (Accessed June 2021).

'Investing in People: How OCBC Bank Unlocks its Employees' Potential', OCBC Bank. eFinancialCareers, 10 January 2019. Available at: https://www.efinancialcareers.sg/news/2019/01/

investing-people-ocbc-bank-unlocks-employees-potential-sc (Accessed June 2021).

Kalra, Aditi Sharma. 'Q&A: Jason Ho, Executive VP and Head of Group HR, OCBC Bank'. *Human Resources Online*, 30 May 2018. Available at: https://www.humanresourcesonline.net/qa-jason-ho-executive-vp-and-head-of-group-hr-ocbc-bank (Accessed June 2021).

'OCBC Bank Awarded The Best HR Initiative, Application or Programme for 2018 at The Asian Banker Financial Technology Innovation Awards 2018'. *The Asian Banker*, 24 May 2018. Available at: https://www.theasianbanker.com/updates-and-articles/ocbc-bank-awarded-the-best-hr-initiative-applicationor-programme-for-2018-at-the-asian-banker-financialtechnology-innovation-awards-2018 (Accessed June 2021).

'OCBC's New HR App Includes AI-powered Chatbot'. *Human Resources Online*, 7 June 2017. Available at: https://www.humanresourcesonline.net/ocbcs-new-hr-app-includes-aipowered-chatbot (Accessed June 2021).

'OCBC Bank's Data Certification Pathway is first data analytics and digital programme to obtain industry accreditation'. Institute of Banking and Finance (IBF) Singapore, 24 August 2020. Available at: https://www.ibf.org.sg/newsroom/Pages/NewsroomDetail.aspx?newsroomid=52&newsroomtypeid=b24530e6-feaa-4334-9708-2da5651f1b32 (Accessed June 2021).

'OCBC Bank Launches Digital Transformation Programme For 29,000 Employees'. *Fintech Singapore*, 8 May 2018. Available at: https://fintechnews.sg/19664/fintech/ocbc-bank-digital-transformation-programme-for-29000-employees/ (Accessed June 2021).

'OCBC Bank Rolls Out Comprehensive Sustainability Training as it Adds More Than 50 New Jobs in ESG Push', 8 July 2021. OCBC Bank. Available at: https://www.ocbc.com/group/media/release/2021/sustainability_training.page? (Accessed June 2021).

Sharma, Anushree. 'OCBC's Head of Group HR, Jason Ho on "Adaptable HR"'. *People Matters*, 23 July 2020. Available at: https://www.peoplemattersglobal.com/article/hr-technology/ocbcs-headof-group-hr-jason-ho-on-adaptable-hr-26426 (Accessed June2021).

'Using Data Analytics and Tech in HR'. The HR Space, 2018. Available at: https://www.thehrspace.com.au/news/using-dataanalytics-and-tech-in-hr/27721/ (Accessed June 2021).

Chapter 8

Cameron, Kim S., and Robert E. Quinn. *Diagnosing and Changing Organizational Culture: Based on The Competing Values Framework.* Third edition. San Francisco: Jossey-Bass, 2011.

Christensen, Clayton M., and Henry J. Eyring. *The Innovative University: Changing the DNA of Higher Education from the Inside Out.* New Jersey: John Wiley & Sons, 2011.

Graham, Dr Ruth. *The Global State of the Art in Engineering Education.* MIT, March 2018. Available at: https://jwel.mit.edu/sites/mit-jwel/files/assets/files/neet_global_state_of_eng_edu_180330.pdf (Accessed October 2021).

Li, Toh Wen. 'NTU, SUTD and A*Star Among Top in World for Research in Various Fields: Study'. *The Straits Times*, 3 October 2017. Available at: https://www.straitstimes.com/singapore/education/ntu-sutd-and-astar-among-top-in-worldfor-research-in-various-fields-study (Accessed October 2021).

Martin, Roger L. *The Opposable Mind: Winning Through Integrative Thinking*. Boston: Harvard Business Press, 2009.

Report of the Committee on the Future Economy, February 2017. Ministry of Trade and Industry. Available at: https://www.mti.gov.sg/-/media/MTI/Resources/Publications/Report-of-the-Committee-on-the-Future-Economy/CFE_Full-Report.pdf (Accessed October 2021).

Whiting, Kate. 'These are the top 10 job skills of tomorrow—and how long it takes to learn them'. World Economic Forum, 21 October 2020. Available at: https://www.weforum.org/agenda/2020/10/top-10-work-skills-of-tomorrow-how-longit-takes-to-learn-them/ (Accessed September 2021).

Chapter 9

Glassdoor Reviews, SAP, 2021. Available at: https://www.glassdoor.sg/Reviews/sap-reviews-SRCH_KE0,3.htm (Accessed October 2021).

'Life at SAP'. Available at: https://www.sap.com/sea/about/careers/who-we-are/life.html (Accessed October 2021).

Lotzmann, Natalie. 'Health and Well-Being Impact the Bottom Line—The Proof Is There!'. Linkedin Pulse, 21 May 2019.

Available at: https://www.linkedin.com/pulse/healthwell-being-impact-bottom-line-proof-dr-natalie-lotzmann/ (Accessed October 2021).

Purcell, Jim, and Steven Van Yoder (ed.). 'Case Study: SAP Shows How Employee Well-being Boosts The Bottom Line'. *Forbes*, 28 October 2019. Available at: https://www.forbes.com/sites/jimpurcell/2019/10/28/case-study-sap-shows-how-employeewellbeing-boosts-the-bottom-line/ (Accessed October 2021).

Raelson, Adam Michael. 'SAP Is Recognized Again As A Best Place to Work, According to Glassdoor 2019 Employees' Choice'. SAP Community, 5 December 2018. Available at: https://blogs.sap.com/2018/12/05/sap-is-recognizedagain-as-a-best-place-to-work-according-to-glassdoor-2019-employees-choice/ (Accessed October 2021).

SAP Integrated Report 2020. Available at: https://www.sap.com/integrated-reports/2020/en.html (Accessed October 2021)

SAP Annual Report 2020, p.40. Available at: https://www.sap.com/docs/download/investors/2020/sap-2020-annualreport-form-20f.pdf (Accessed October 2021).

Thomasson, Emma.'At Germany's SAP, Employee Mindfulness Leads to Higher Profits'. Reuters, 17 May 2018. Available at: https://www.reuters.com/article/us-world-worksap-idUSKCN1II1BW (Accessed October 2021).

Chapter 10

'About SkillsFuture'. SkillsFuture SG, 6 August 2021. Available at: https://www.skillsfuture.gov.sg/AboutSkillsFuture (Accessed September 2021).

Baig, Aamer, Bryce Hall, Paul Jenkins, Eric Lamarre and Brian McCarthy. 'The COVID-19 Recovery Will Be Digital: A Plan for the First 90 Days'. McKinsey, 14 May 2020. Available at: https://www.mckinsey.com/business-functions/mckinseydigital/our-insights/the-covid-19-recovery-will-be-digital-aplan-for-the-first-90-days (Accessed October 2021).

Bersin, Josh. 'New Research Shows Why Focus On Teams, Not Just Leaders, Is Key To Business Performance'. *Forbes*, 3 March 2016. Available at: https://www.forbes.com/sites/joshbersin/2016/03/03/why-a-focus-on-teams-not-just-leadersis-the-secret-to-business-performance/?sh=77eab05f24d5 (Accessed September 2021).

Bezamat, Felipe. 'This is the Key to Manufacturing in a Postpandemic World'. World Economic Forum, 17 November 2020. Available at: https://www.weforum.org/agenda/2020/11/this-is-the-key-to-manufacturing-in-a-post-pandemic-world/ (Accessed October 2021).

'Big Data', *The Infinite Monkey Cage with Brian Cox and Robin Ince* [podcast]. *BBC* Series 18, 16 July 2018. Available at: https://www.bbc.co.uk/programmes/b0b9wbf8 (Accessed July 2021).

Chesbrough, Henry, and Marcel Bogers. 'Explicating Open Innovation: Clarifying an Emerging Paradigm for Understanding

Innovation', in Henry Chesbrough, Wim Vanhaverbeke, and Joel West (Eds.). *New Frontiers in Open Innovation*. Oxford: Oxford University Press, 2014. pp. 3–28.

Chesbrough, Henry. 'Everything You Need to Know about Open Innovation'. *Forbes*, 11 March 2011. Available at: https://www.forbes.com/sites/henrychesbrough/2011/03/21/everything-you-need-to-know-about-open-innovation/ (Accessed September 2021).

Choy, Natalie. "OCBC Bank, "OCBC Rolls Out Sustainability Training for Staff as Part of S\$30m Skills Drive". Banking and Finance, July 8, 2021. Available at: https://www.businesstimes.com.sg/banking-finance/ocbc-rolls-out-sustainability-training-forstaff-as-part-of-s30m-skills-drive (Accessed September 2021).

Crama, Pascale, Chon Phung Lim, Cintia Kulzer Sacilotto, and Jovina Ang. 'Innovating Singapore's Chicken Rice', Teaching Note: Singapore Management University, SMU-20-0050, February 2021.

'Coming soon: AirAsia's First Ever Airvolution Hackathon!'. AirAsia, 16 January 2017. Available at: https://ir.airasia.com/news.html/id/627977 (Accessed September 2021).

Dawkins, Tim. 'How COVID-19 Could Open the Door for Driverless Deliveries'. World Economic Forum, 7 April 2020. Available at: https://www.weforum.org/agenda/2020/04/how-covid-19-could-open-the-door-for-driverless-deliveries/ (Accessed October 2021).

D'Onfro, Jillian. "The Truth About Google's Famous '20% Time' Policy". Business Insider, April 18, 2015. Available at: https://www.businessinsider.com/google-20-per cent-time-policy-2015-4 (Accessed September 2021).

'Digital Transformation Series: Satya Nadella on Digital Transformation for Microsoft'[video], YouTube, posted by Centre of Executive Education, 28 July 2020. Available at: https://www.youtube.com/watch?v=_zgSSeZJH30 (Accessed March 2021).

Dixon, Michael. 'How Netflix Used Big Data and Analytics to Generate Billions'. Selerity, April 5, 2019. Available at: https://seleritysas.com/blog/2019/04/05/how-netflix-used-big-dataand-analytics-to-generate-billions (Accessed July 2021).

Expert Panel of the Forbes Human Resources Council, '15 Effective Ways HR Teams Can Leverage Big Data'. *Forbes*, 2 February 2021. Available at: https://www.forbes.com/sites/forbeshumanresourcescouncil/2021/02/02/15-effective-ways-hrteams-can-leverage-big-data/ (Accessed September 2021).

Feder, Barnaby J. 'At Motorola, Quality Is a Team Sport'. *The New York Times*, 21 January, 1993. Available at: https://www.nytimes.com/1993/01/21/business/at-motorola-quality-is-ateam-sport.html (Accessed September 2021).

For more information on the altMBA programme, please see: https://altmba.com/faq#what-is-the-curriculum (Accessed September 2021).

'Grab. Making Everyday Better'. Grab, 2021. Available at: https://www.grab.com/sg/ (Accessed October 2021).

Gowing, Nik, and Chris Langdon. 'The New GANDALF: "How to Ensure the Switch Goes On"', *Thinking the Unthinkable*. Woodbridge: John Catt Educational Ltd, 2018. Available at: https://www.thinkunthink.org/perch/resources/documents/ttudbsbankchapter.pdf (Accessed September 2021).

Goldsmith, Marshall. *What Got You Here Won't Get You There: How Successful People Become Even More Successful*. New York: Hyperion, 2007.

Gumbel, Peter, and Angelika Reich. "Building the Workforce of Tomorrow, Today". McKinsey Quarterly. Available at: https://www.mckinsey.com/business-functions/organization/our-insights/building-theworkforce-of-tomorrow-today (Accessed September 2021).

Helper, Susan, and Evan Soltas, 'Why the Pandemic Has Disrupted Supply Chains'. The White House, 17 June 2021. Available at: https://www.whitehouse.gov/cea/blog/2021/06/17/why-thepandemic-has-disrupted-supply-chains/ (Accessed October 2021).

'How Companies are Using Big Data and Analytics'. McKinsey, 21 April 2016. Available at: https://www.mckinsey.com/business-functions/mckinsey-analytics/ourinsights/how-companies-are-using-big-data-and-analytics (Accessed September 2021).

Ibarra, Herminia. *Act Like a Leader, Think Like a Leader*. Boston: Harvard Business Review Press, 2015. p.4.

Kartha, Suvarna. 'SAP Labs India—Indeed, A Great Place to Work!—My Story'. LinkedIn, 21 August 2019. Available at: https://www.linkedin.com/pulse/sap-labs-india-indeed-great-place-workmy-story-suvarna-kartha-1d (Accessed September 2021).

Kleckler, Abby. 'People Counting Technology Beyond COVID-19'. Progressive Grocer, 4 May 2020. Available at: https://progressivegrocer.com/people-counting-technologybeyond-covid-19 (Accessed October 2021).

Lim, Jamilah 'What Will it Take to Bridge the Digital Skills Gap in APAC?'. *Techwire Asia*, 25 August 2021. Available at: https://techwireasia.com/2021/08/what-will-it-take-to-bridge-thedigital-skills-gap-in-apac/ (Accessed September 2021).

Mims, Christopher. "The '20% Time' Perk at Google Is No More". *The Atlantic*, August 16, 2013. Available at: https://www.theatlantic.com/technology/archive/2013/08/20-time-perk-google-nomore/312063/ (Accessed September 2021).

"New World New Skills", 2020. Price Waterhouse Coopers (PwC). Available at: https://www.pwc.com/sg/en/publications/new-worldnew-skills.html (Accessed September 2021).

"OCBC Bank Launches the Largest Workforce Digital Transformation Programme for 29,000 employees". OCBC Bank. May 8, 2018. Available at: https://www.ocbc.com/group/media/release/2018/ocbc-future-smart-programme.page (Accessed September 2021).

Perry, Philip.'47% of Jobs Will Vanish in the Next 25 Years, Say Oxford University Researchers'. Big Think, 24 December 2016.

Available at: https://bigthink.com/philip-perry/47-ofjobs-in-the-next-25-years-will-disappear-according-to-oxforduniversity (Accessed July 2021).

Price, Dominic. "What is a Culture of Innovation?". Inside Atlassian, April 7, 2019. Available at: https://www.atlassian.com/blog/inside-atlassian/how-to-build-culture-of-innovation-every-day (Accessed September 2021).

"'Queen Bee" Firms to Mobilise Other Employers to Uplift Their Sectors' Capabilities: Lawrence Wong'. *Channel News Asia*, 21 January 2021. Available at: https://www.channelnewsasia.com/business/singapore-industry-workforce-lawrence-wongskillsfuture-423231. (Accessed September 2021).

Schaper, Michael T. 'There are more than 70 million micro-, small- and mediumsized enterprises (SMEs) in Southeast Asia'. 'The Missing (Small) Businesses of Southeast Asia'. Yusok Ishak Institute, No. 79, 22 July 2020. Available at: https://www.iseas.edu.sg/wp-content/uploads/2020/06/ISEAS_Perspective_2020_79.pdf (Accessed September 2021).

Shilcock, Amanda Bergson. "Boosting Digital Literacy in the Workplace". National Skills Coalition, December 15, 2020. Available at: https://www.nationalskillscoalition.org/wp-content/uploads/2021/01/12152020-NSC-Boosting-Digital-Literacy.pdf (Accessed September 2021).

'Startup Day at La Maison des Startups LVMH at Station F Accelerates Collaboration between LVMH Maisons and New Tech Businesses'. LVMH, 9 December 2019. Available at: https://www.lvmh.com/news-documents/news/startupday-at-la-maison-des-startups-lvmh-at-station-f-acceleratescollaboration-between-lvmh-maisons-and-new-techbusinesses/(Accessed September 2021).

Station F at LVMH, 'New at STATION F! Meet LVMH's LuxuryTech Startups'. *Medium*, 19 April 2018. Available at: https://medium.com/station-f/new-at-station-f-meet-lvmhsluxurytech-startups-b4fc5136241e (Accessed September 2021).

Sweeney, Erica. 'L'Oréal, General Assembly Create New Assessment for Digital Marketers'. *Marketing Dive*, 13 November 2018. Available at: https://www.marketingdive.com/news/loreal-general-assembly-create-new-assessment-for-digitalmarketers/542071/ (Accessed September 2021).

Tan, Sumiko. 'Lunch With Sumiko: No such thing as a silly idea, says billionaire inventor James Dyson'. *The Straits Times*, 5 September 2021. Available at: https://www.straitstimes.com/singapore/lunch-with-sumiko-no-such-thing-as-a-silly-ideasays-billionaire-inventor-james-dyson (Accessed September 2021).

Ting, Yong Hui. "Shopee to Help SMEs Upskill via SkillsFuture Queen Bee Programme". The Business Times, March 31, 2021. Available at: https://www.businesstimes.com.sg/sme/shopee-to-helpsmes-upskill-via-skillsfuture-queen-bee-programme (Accessed September 2021).

Thomke, Stefan. "Building a Culture of Experimentation". Harvard Business Review, March-April 2020. Available at: https://hbr.org/2020/03/building-a-culture-of-experimentation (Accessed September 2021).

Tonby, Oliver, Li-Kai Chen and Anu Madgavkar. 'Tackling Asia's Talent Challenge: How to Adapt to a Digital Future'. McKinsey, 26 July 2021. Available at: https://www.mckinsey.com/featuredinsights/asia-pacific/tackling-asias-talent-challenge-how-toadapt-to-a-digital-future (Accessed September 2021).

'Tony Fernandes Talks AirAsia's Digital Arline Roadmap for 2017, Upcoming CVC & Accelerator', 19 March 2017. TechSauce. Available at: https://techsauce.co/tech-and-biz/tonyfernandes-talks-airasia-digital-airline-roadmap-2017 (Accessed September 2021).

Tullis, Jonathzn G., and Aaron S. Benjamin. 'On the Effectiveness of Learning'. *J Mem Lang*, 64, no.2, 1 February 2011, p.109–188. Available at: 10.1016/j.jml.2010.11.002 (Accessed September 2021).

United Women Singapore. 'Distinguished Speaker Series Featuring Piyush Gupta', 11 September 2021. Available at: https://uws.org.sg/distinguished-speaker-series-september-2021/(Accessed July 2021).

Vries, James de. 'PepsiCo's Chief Design Officer on Creating an Organization Where Design Can Thrive'. *Harvard Business Review*, 11 August 2015. Available at: https://hbr.org/2015/08/pepsicos-chief-design-officer-on-creating-an-organizationwhere-design-can-thrive (Accessed September 2021).

"Who We are", 2021. Atlassian. Available at: https://www.atlassian.com/company (Accessed September 2021).

Yu, Eileen. 'Cloud, Data Amongst APAC Digital Skills Most Needed'. *ZDNet*, 25 February 2021. Available at: https://www.

zdnet.com/article/cloud-data-amongst-apac-digital-skillsmost-needed/ (Accessed September 2021).

Wilkinson, Angela, and Roland Kupers. 'Living in the Futures'. *Harvard Business Review*, May 2013. Available at: https://hbr.org/2013/05/living-in-the-futures (Accessed September 2021).

'What are Shell Scenarios?' Shell, n.d.m. Available at: https://www.shell.com/energy-and-innovation/the-energy-future/scenarios/what-are-scenarios.html (Accessed September 2021).

Chapter 11

Agarwal, Sumit. 'Commentary: The Gig Economy—a Surprise Boost from the Pandemic and in Singapore, it's not Going Anywhere'. *Channel News Asia*, 9 March 2021. Available at: https://www.channelnewsasia.com/news/commentary/gig-economyperformance-covid-19-jobs-revenue-grab-gojek-14288764 (Accessed July 2021).

Alawadhi, Neha.'Satya Nadella: A History Buff in School, says Sachin Yesterday, Virat Today'. *Business Standard*, 27 February 2020. Available at: https://www.business-standard.com/article/companies/satya-nadella-a-history-buff-in-school-sayssachin-yesterday-virat-today-120022600599_1.html (Accessed September 2021).

Carter, Rebekah. 'The Role of AR in the Future of Work', *XR Today*, 30 April 2021. Available at: https://www.xrtoday.com/augmented-reality/the-role-of-ar-in-the-future-of-work/ (Accessed October 2021).

Dillon, Karen. 'Disruption 2020: An Interview With Clayton M. Christensen'. *MIT Sloan Management Review*, Spring 2020. Available at: ttps://sloanreview.mit.edu/article/an-interviewwith-clayton-m-christensen/ (Accessed September 2021).

European Observatory of Working Life, 'Platform Work'. Eurofound, 29 June 2018. Available at: https://www.eurofound.europa.eu/observatories/eurwork/industrial-relationsdictionary/platform-work (Accessed October 2021).

Engelbert, Cathy, and John Hagel. 'Radically Open: Tom Friedman on Jobs, Learning and the Future of Work'. Deloitte Insights, July 2017. Available at: https://www2.deloitte.com/content/dam/insights/us/articles/3932_Radically-open/DUP_Radically-open-reprint.pdf (Accessed October 2021).

Gallagher, James. 'Remarkable Decline in Fertility Rates', *BBC*, 9 November 2018. Available at: https://www.bbc.com/news/health-46118103 (Accessed August 2021).

Gray, Alex. 'This is What's Worrying CEOs the Most'. World Economic Forum, 29 January 2016. Available at: https://www.weforum.org/agenda/2016/01/this-is-what-s-worrying-ceos/ (Accessed October 2021).

Greenwood, Peter Evans, Harvey Lewis, and James Guszcza. 'Reconstructing Work: Automation, Artificial Intelligence and the Essential Role of Humans'. *Deloitte Review*, Issue 21, July 2017. Available at: https://www2.deloitte.com/content/dam/insights/us/articles/3883_Reconstructing-work/DUP_Reconstructing-work-reprint.pdf (Accessed October 2021).

Ghoshal, Somak. 'HarperCollins Publishers India Will Grant 'Pawternity Leave' To Employees Adopting Pets'. *Huffington Post*, 6 April 2017. Available at: https://www.huffpost.com/archive/in/entry/harpercollins-publishers-india-will-grantpawternity-leave-to_a_22028162 (Accessed October 2021).

Hameed, Naumaan. 'Geopolitical Impact on Global Immigration', KPMG, May 2019. Available at: https://home.kpmg/xx/en/home/insights/2019/05/geopolitical-impacton-global-immigration.html (Accessed September 2021).

Hastwell, Claire. 'Top 5 Things Millennials Want in the Workplace in 2021'. Great Place to Work, 16 July 2021. Available at: https://www.greatplacetowork.com/resources/blog/top-5-things-millennials-want-in-the-workplace-in-2021-as-told-by-millennials?utm_source=website_bw_millenials&utm_medium=promoted&utm_campaign=bwmillenials2021&utm_content=gptw_rhc (Accessed October 2021).

'How It Works'. Upwork, 2021. Available at: https://www.upwork.com/i/how-it-works/client/ (Accessed October 2021).

Intuit, *Intuit 2020 Report*, October 2010. Available at: http://http-download.intuit.com/http.intuit/CMO/intuit/futureofsmallbusiness/intuit_2020_report.pdf?_ga=1.82600086.1286327959.1409610840 (Accessed October 2021).

Iwamoto, Kentaro. 'Local Jobs or Global Talent? Singapore Faces COVID-era Conundrum'. *Nikkei Asia*, 3 November 2020. Available at: https://asia.nikkei.com/Spotlight/Asia-Insight/Local-jobs-or-global-talent-Singapore-faces-COVIDera-conundrum (Accessed September 2021).

Khanna, Parag. *Move: The Forces Uprooting Us.* New York: Scribner, 2021.

'Life in 2025: what will the future look like?'. *Financial Times*, 16 December 2020. Available at: https://www.ft.com/content/25ccd513-6b95-4596-a9d6-a74764fb3dc1 (Accessed October 2021).

Manyika, James, Susan Lund, Michael Chui, Jacques Bughin, Jonathan Woetzel, Parul Batra, Ryan Ko, and Saurabh Sanghvi. 'Jobs Lost, Jobs Gained: What the Future of Work will Mean for Jobs, Skills, and Wages'. McKinsey Global Institute, 28 November 2017. Available at: https://www.mckinsey.com/featured-insights/future-of-work/jobs-lost-jobs-gainedwhat-the-future-of-work-will-mean-for-jobs-skills-and-wages (Accessed October 2021).

Ranger, Steve. 'Microsoft CEO Satya Nadella: The whole world is now a computer'. *ZDnet*, 22 May 2018. Available at: https://www.zdnet.com/article/microsoft-ceo-nadella-the-wholeworld-is-now-a-computer/ (Accessed October 2021).

Richter, Felix. 'COVID-19 has Caused a Huge Amount of Lost Working Hours'. World Economic Forum, 4 February 2021. Available at: https://www.weforum.org/agenda/2021/02/covid-employment-global-job-loss/ (Accessed July 2021).

Schwartz, Jeff, Heather Stockton, and Kelly Monahan. 'Forces of Change'. The Future of Work Series, Deloitte Insights, July 2017. Available at: https://www2.deloitte.com/content/dam/insights/us/articles/4322_Forces-of-change_FoW/DI_Forces-of-change_FoW.pdf (Accessed September 2021).

'SAP Next Talent', SAP, 2021. Available at: https://www.sap.com/sea/about/careers/students-graduates/graduates/nexttalent. html (Accessed October 2021).

'The Future of Human Geography'[video], YouTube, posted by Parag Khanna, 17 June 2021. Av https://www.youtube.com/watch?v=FKexILzphoI (Accessed August 2021).

UiPath, 'Study Finds Nearly 50% of Businesses Around the World Will Increase Robotic Process Automation Adoption due to COVID-19'. *Business Wire*, 28 July 2020. Available at: https://www.businesswire.com/news/home/20200728005136/en/Study-Finds-Nearly-50-of-Businesses-Around-the-World-Will-Increase-Robotic-Process-Automation-Adoption-due-to-COVID-19 (Accessed October 2021).

Wiley Education Services and Future Workplace, 'New Study Reveals Skills Gap Grew By Double Digits Since Last Year'. *Business Wire*, 4 September 2019. Available at: https://www.businesswire.com/news/home/20190904005094/en/New-Study-Reveals-Skills-Gap-Grew-By-Double-Digits-Since-Last-Year (Accessed September 2021).

Index

F

failures 51, 53, 59, 149, 195, 208; Hogen on 60
Fernandes, Tony 9, 197
Finastra 34
fluidity 19, 42, 142
Food Innovation and Resource Centre (FIRC) 201
Fourth Industrial Revolution 10, 140, 220
Fralinger, Barbara 15
Franklin, Daniel 20, 66
Freda, Fabrizio 55
Fry, Hannah 204
full-time employees 40
Future Economy 68, 140

G

Gartner 37; recommendations of 43–44
Gates, Bill 51
General Electric (GE) 63, 206, 215
generational groups 210
geopolitics xiv, 208, 214–16, 226
Gino, Francesca 12–13
Glassdoor 162, 173
Global Financial Crisis 57, 221
global talent pool 77
goals 15, 18, 45, 57, 88–89, 104, 108, 113, 188
Goldsmith, Marshall 175
Google 27, 46, 76, 103, 195; Hangouts 26, 28; Project Oxygen 76, 88, 103; X Lab 196
Goran, Julie 13
Great Lockdown 1, 24, 176, 222
Great Place to Work 35, 211
'The Great Resignation' 1–3, *see also* attrition
greenhouse gas emissions 71, *see also* climate change
Griffin, Jane 90